Selected Hutterian Documents
IN TRANSLATION
1542 - 1654

JOHN A. HOSTETLER
LEONARD GROSS & ELIZABETH BENDER

© 2013 Hutterian Brethren Book Centre.
First printed in 1975 by the Communal Studies Centre,
Temple University, Philadelphia, Pa.

Canadian spelling conventions have been adopted in this edition.

Box 40 • MacGregor, MB • R0H 0R0 • Canada
P. 204-272-5132 • F. 204-252-2381

Cover design: Yvonne Parks

Habaner motif: © Jan Glaysteen. Used by permission.

ISBN 978-0-9865381-9-3

Library and Archives Canada Cataloguing in Publication

Hutterian Brethren
[Works. Selections. English. 2013]
    Selected Hutterian documents in translation, 1542-1654 / [translated by]
John A. Hostetler, Leonard Gross & Elizabeth Bender.

Translated from the German.
Reprint. Originally published: Philadelphia : Communal Studies Center,
    Temple University, 1975.
Includes bibliographical references.
ISBN 978-0-9865381-9-3 (pbk.)

    1. Hutterian Brethren--Doctrines. I. Hostetler, John A. (John Andrew),
1918-, translator II. Gross, Leonard, 1931 November 17-, translator
III. Bender, Elizabeth, 1895-1988, translator IV. Hutterian Brethren Book
Centre V. Title.

BX8129.H8H88 2013   230'.973   C2013-903373-4

Printed and bound in Canada.

CONTENTS

INTRODUCTION I

CONCERNING THE UPBRINGING OF CHILDREN 1
    Peter Riedemann, "Concerning the Upbringing
    of children" ca. 11 1542 1
    The Address Which Brother Peter Walpot, Together with
    Other [Elders] Delivered to the Schoolmasters at
    Nemschitz (Němčice), November 15, 1568 2
    School Management Code to be Discussed
    with the School Personnel, 1568, 1578 6
    Claus Braidl, 1588 (School Management Code Addenda) 15
    Address…to the Schoolmasters, January 9, 1596 16

A SIXTEENTH-CENTURY HUTTERIAN
CATECHISM FOR CHILDREN 21
    God and His Creation 21
    Concerning Faith 24
    Concerning Prayer 28
    On Christian Baptism 29
    On the Lord's Supper 30
    On Christian Avoidance 31
    On the Training of Children 31

TWO SERMONS ON BAPTISM AND THE ACCOMPANYING
FORMULAE (TAUFREDEN) 33
    THE FIRST ADDRESS 33
    One Almighty God 34
    God Created Man for That Purpose 35
    God Created Man in His Image 36
    Man Forsook the Image of God When he Fell into Sin 37

Sin 38
Original Sin 39
To What Extent Original Sin is Harmful 40
The Course and Life of This World 40
God's Wrath, Curse, Punishment, and Judgment 48
BEGINNING OR INTRODUCTION
TO THE SECOND ADDRESS 50
SECOND ADDRESS 50
[Man Must] Acknowledge his Sins 50
Repentance and Sorrow for Sin 51
True Repentance and Reformation 52
Faith 54
Grafted and Incorporated into Christ 55
Assured, Sealed and Empowered by His Spirit 56
Gospel 57
New Testament 57
Commission 59
Separation.. 59
Mortification 61
Yieldedness (*Gelassenheit*) 61
Christian Community [of Goods] 63
Submission (*Ergebung*) 67
Obedience 68
To the True Christian Baptism 69
Supper of the Lord.. 71
Cross of Christ... 73
Questions to be Asked Those Who Have Yielded Themselves 74
Questions to be Asked When Baptism is to Take Place 75
FIRST ADDRESS (AN ALTERNATE VERSION) 76

**REGULATION CONCERNING THE MATCHING OF THE
YOUNG PEOPLE FOR MARRIAGE, 1643, Andreas Ehrenpreis**........ 89
    APPENDIX: Sources Concerning the Traditional Marriage
    Practices of the Hutterites (Compiled by Robert Friedmann)............. 95

**THE COMMUNAL DISCIPLINE OF 1651:
Annual Exhortation of the Faithful Brethren** 97

THE BARBER-SURGEON ("BADER") DISCIPLINE OF 1654 113

INTRODUCTION

This publication embodies a number of the earlier communal disciplines of the Hutterian Brethren written during a time-span of more than a century, beginning with the first generation of the Hutterian movement (1542), and continuing into the late Ehrenpreis era (1654). The handful of documents included here is a mere sample of the broad-ranging spectrum of Hutterian documents; for there is a vast segment of Hutterian history and culture to be probed in the many European archives which house the sixteenth and seventeenth century collections of Hutterian Anabaptistica.

The scope and variety of these hundreds of codices and writings continues to astonish even the long-time scholar of Hutterianism. (See the catalogue of manuscripts in European libraries and archives compiled by the late Robert Friedmann and Adolf Mais, *Die Schriften der huterischen Täufergemeinschaften: Gesamtkatalog ihrer Manuskriptbücher, ihrer Schreiber und ihrer Literatur, 1529-1667* [Vienna, 1965].)

The selected documents in this publication are a gesture toward the larger task of publishing in German, and in English translation, all of the communal disciplines in a single volume. It is hoped that in the near future this will be accomplished. The documents below were too voluminous to include in two recent books (though utilized in their preparation), namely, John A. Hostetler, *Hutterite Society* (Baltimore, Md.: Johns Hopkins University Press, 1974), and Leonard Gross, *The Golden Years of the Hutterites: The Witness and Thought of the Communal Moravian Anabaptists During the Walpot Era, 1565-1578* (Ann Arbor, Mich.: University Microfilms [# 75-19,967], 1975, also forthcoming in a hardcover edition). These documents are offered in this limited edition to those who during the coming years wish to pursue Hutterian social and cultural history and its religious thought. The documents below, representative of the larger corpus of materials, will hopefully be useful in charting the evolution of idea and life within Hutterianism through 1650.

A few comments about the documents will help set the distinct change which affected Hutterian life directly, as the Brotherhood attempted to maintain its faith, outer change notwithstanding.

The first section, "Concerning the Upbringing of Children," holds special significance in that the unit forms a major section of a pedagogical codex compiled by *Vorsteher* Claus Braidl, coordinating head of the entire Hutterian Brotherhood of some 20,000 souls. Braidl began the writing in 1593, and completed the codex in 1596. Here the whole spectrum of Hutterian education of children is presented, beginning with the (*ca.*) 1542 writing of Peter Riedemann on the upbringing of children, to the 1568 and 1578 documents of *Vorsteher* Peter Walpot and Hans Král, and finally including the documents which suggest something of the school problems in the late 1580s and '90s. Here we have the whole range of the history of Hutterian schools brought together into one document, composed at the end of the Golden Era of early Hutterianism, just preceding the tragic and coercive breakup of the whole of Moravian (Hutterian) Anabaptism. Other such documents in Hutterian codices will need to be compared to search for possible addenda to this "Codex Braidl," but for our purposes this one codex will help to measure change within the long Hutterian movement, at least through the 1590s. After that point political disruptions forced change from without, in addition to the internal development of idea and circumstance.

Although the school problems during the 1540s through the 1570s were certainly difficult to solve, the approach of the whole Brotherhood in general, and the leadership in particular, suggests a fine balance struck in attempting to cope with perennial problems within the schools, highly innovative for their times. The manner of dealing with problems reflects the Hutterian conception of the nature of children; the spirit and effectiveness in dealing with children also provides deep insights into the nature of Hutterian communal life. Much care and consensus went into the solving of these problems; the same care and diligence is written into the 1542 and the 1568/78 documents. However, by 1588 and 1596 a new mood demands, it seems, different approaches; the 1570s are already a bygone "golden age," and the profundity of the Hutterian way in its pure state already seems to be waning.

[...] Since 1931, when the English translation by Harold S. Bender of the 1568 Address of Peter Walpot and the 1578 School Management Code appeared (see the *Mennonite Quarterly Review*, V [October 1931], 231-44), several new codices of these and similar materials have come to light (e.g., Brno, ČSSR, and Rifton, N.Y.). These still await careful comparison and analysis.

The beautiful catechism for children (pp. 49-62 below), lifted from a small pedagogical codex at Olomouc, ČSSR, suggests the depth of the Hutterites' concern for teaching the children who have not yet been baptized; they are still to be brought up in the fear of God and taught respect and appreciation for all of God's creation, but especially for the Brotherhood-Church (*Gemeinde*), which God established and which the Hutterites were faithfully continuing in their response to God as His People. The language of this catechism, although simple, communicates the subtleties of the Hutterian way of life, and their approach to God's Truth. The interpretive and poetic approach to conceiving God's creation, and how man is to respond, is the work of a mature and perceptive writer, and although the catechism is undated, it seems to fit the Walpot or Kräl period (1565-83).

The *Taufreden* (baptismal sermons)—as presented below—are unique among those extant in Hutterian literature in that they are the only known, full-length sermons which were not only written in the sixteenth century, but are taken from a sixteenth century codex (1599). But again, the internal evidence not only makes clear that the sermons are pre-1593 (see p. 115). but that they most probably were also originally written during the Walpot-Kräl era, when the mood of the times demanded this rather highly interpretive approach to teaching and worship. The alternate version of the First Address, presented after the baptismal formulae (pp. 118ff) on the other hand emanates a highly different mood, and is more in line with seventeenth century writings, where communicating biblical truth closely follows the original biblical textual materials, chapter by chapter.

Of the various forms of the *Taufreden* known to us, including the modern versions used by the Hutterites today, these are the most highly interpretive, even better in style than the so-called "1584 version," discovered in Sobotiste, ČSSR in 1961, only partially extant (see Friedmann, *Schriften*, 162-63 for further analysis). The original writer develops here an explicit confession of faith and sense of history, an acknowledgment of God's movement within history of which the Hutterites are an integral part. Herein lies meaning for the Hutterites, and for their mission and witness, and hence also in baptism, which is the crucial point where an individual becomes a brother or sister, relating closely to other brethren and so sharing together in God's covenant. This profound document will merit further analysis and interpretation in the coming years.

The "Regulation Concerning the Matching of the Young People for Marriage" (1643), the "Communal Discipline" (1651), and the "Barber-Surgeon Discipline" (1654) represent a later period of Hutterian life. All show the intensifying of external problems, internal deterioration of leadership, and methods that were harsher and less diplomatic than sixteenth century practice. Certainly the political upheaval of 1593ff, and especially 1618ff (the Thirty Years War) uprooted absolutely the greatest majority of the Hutterian *Haushaben* (communal groups). Simply to attempt to hold together the Hutterian remnant was in itself a major task and the greatest of challenges. Furthermore, the sixteenth century concept of mission and witness came to an end, and a type of cultural fixation set in, determining rigid outward patterns of living and dress.

The translation of these documents was made possible by a grant from the National Institutes of Mental Health, for which the senior editor is deeply grateful. Leonard Gross (Executive Secretary of the Mennonite Historical Committee, Goshen, Indiana) provided technical and editorial skills and Elizabeth Horsch Bender (Goshen) translated and rendered valuable counsel in producing this publication. Ilse Reist (Scottdale, Pennsylvania) assisted in the initial translation of the three last sources. Elizabeth Hershberger Bauman (Goshen) typed the final manuscript.

CONCERNING THE UPBRINGING OF CHILDREN, REGULATION FOR SCHOOLS, AND MATTERS TO BE DISCUSSED WITH THE PEOPLE ENGAGED IN SCHOOLS; ALSO, AND ESPECIALLY, WITH THE SCHOOLMASTERS

1593

Clauss Braidl

P[eter] R[iedemann], "Concerning the Upbringing of Children," From our *Rechenschafft*

"You parents," says Paul, "do not provoke your children to anger, but bring them up in the discipline and admonition of the Lord." The object of our child training is therefore not to allow them their wantonness and carnal practices.

For that reason we have schools in those places where there is enough space (as in Moravia), where we give our children godly training and teach them from youth or childhood to know God. But we do not let them go to other schools, because they carry on only worldly wisdom, knowledge and practice, and are silent about godly things.

This is how it is done among us: as soon as the mother has weaned her child she gives it to the school, where there are appointed sisters recognized as competent by the brotherhood who take care of them; and as soon as they are able to talk they put the Word of the testimony of God into the child's mouth and teach him to read with or from it, instruct them in prayer in a manner that the child can understand it. The children remain with them until the fifth or sixth year, until they are mature enough to learn to read and write.

When they have reached that stage they are transferred into the care of the schoolmaster, who teaches them these things and instructs them further and further in the knowledge of God, so that they may know God and his will and learn to strive and to keep him in their minds.

He brings them to order in the morning; when they have all arrived he has them thank and pray to the Lord in unison.

Then he begins to give them a half hour's children's sermon: how they are to obey and be submissive to their parents, their taskmasters and superiors and honour them, and pictures for them from the Old and New Testaments the favours and promises for the good children, and on the other hand the punishment for the disobedient and wilful.

From such obedience to parents he teaches them obedience to God and to do his will, and that they should all look up to him as their all-powerful Father, and love, honour, worship and attach themselves to him above all others; yes, serve only him, from whom they have all good things. Thus we teach our children from childhood not to seek temporal things but the eternal. They stay with the schoolmaster until they reach an age when they can learn to work. In whatever type of work each one is seen to be fit and capable, he is held to it.

When they have thus been raised and have learned to know and believe God they are baptized upon the confession of their faith.

THE ADDRESS WHICH BROTHER PETER WALPOT, TOGETHER WITH OTHER [ELDERS] DELIVERED TO THE SCHOOLMASTERS AT NEMSCHITZ, NOVEMBER 15, 1568

Dear Brethren: We have thought it good to call you together and discuss with you the work of the office which has been assigned to you in the schools, so that you might exercise more diligence to care for the children who have been entrusted to us and to you by the Lord and that you may direct their minds to the honour and fear of God, so that they may be brought up for the Lord and may from the time of their youth be restrained from evil.

We therefore desire that you should not engage in other activities that are not entrusted to you, and which would occupy your time; you should stay in the schoolroom with the children. Nor should the managers (*Haushalter*) send you to some other task unless it should be for an hour or two and the task could so on be performed; then each shall return to the children.

They shall not leave the sisters alone with the children. You should not depend upon the sisters and the assistants, for the assistants at times show favouritism in reporting misconduct, when they themselves are likely to have been involved. This gives the sisters occasion to begin to argue with them, because they have much to complain about, especially with the boys; but if a schoolmaster is in the school room among the children and frequently observes them and quiets them, they will become more circumspect and saved from the rod.

Nothing is accomplished by severe beatings; that is, the rod is not to be applied hard and long, although teachers often have, and desire to have, a reputation of this sort. I do not mean, of course, my brethren, that the children can take care of themselves, that there is enough of the fear of God in them to keep them from wrongdoing, for if this were the case a schoolmaster would not be needed.

Furthermore, the schoolmaster is to be present in the school room not only for the children's sake, but also in order to give aid and advice to the sisters, for they need your oversight just as much as the children—since women are women and the weaker vessel—lest they in their annoyance and complaints go about among the children with rods, as one does among cattle, when the flesh gets the upper hand and quickly becomes angry, as we have ourselves experienced. A schoolmaster who is diligent can, with the help of God, prevent such occurrences if he takes his responsibility toward the children as seriously as if they were his own.

Further, dear brethren, when you are at table together with the sisters, you should be properly quiet, not boisterous or conversing about matters which are not profitable or edifying, as commonly is the case if one does not take proper care to give a good example to the children who hear and see such things. For the children quickly observe this and say: What they forbid us they themselves do.

The same care should be taken by the sisters in their brushing. If the sisters are not of one mind, if they contradict each other, if one talks much about another, the young girls notice it and repeat it to one another and consequently will look down on the one spoken of. And not only that, but if for good reason a schoolmaster enquires: "Dear sisters, how about this matter?" and gives his opinion and although his counsel is the better, it does not agree with the sister's ideas, she flares up: "How dare you enquire of this or that; it is not your business," and treats him disrespectfully. Such conduct should not be disregarded, for the children see and hear such things, and become stubborn. Besides, when complaints come, whether in matters of food and drink, clothing, lying down, going to bed, bathing, washing, or service—in whatever form the complaints take, the schoolmaster is ultimately held responsible. If he is able to give a good account of himself, he fares well, and this is the reason that we are pointing this out to you, since there are some of your number who have not been in the school work very long and are not acquainted with our customs, and some school-mothers, especially the older ones, are not willing to give up their old ways or surrender the authority which they have acquired, and this intimidates the brother (schoolmaster).

It has indeed often been the case that parents come to us and say: "My brethren, I have committed myself and my children to the Lord and to the school," and then complain that one of the children has gotten impetigo in the school or some other ailment, be it on the eyes or the hands or the feet. And then if we speak in school or to the schoolmaster about the matter and call him to account, the schoolmaster shifts responsibility to the school-mother, the school-mother to the sisters, bedroom maids, or the nursemaids, although they know that the schoolmaster was responsible. Therefore the schoolmaster shall take good care of the children.

Perhaps the school-mother has at her disposal a nurse maid whom she sends to the sick children in their rooms with food and drink; she depends on her and then the children are badly tended; possibly one is so weak that it does not eat and must wait from one meal to another without food or drink, especially if he does not like what is sent. For such reasons, we say to you, that you yourselves should supervise and tell the sisters that they themselves must also look after the sick ones and ask (in the kitchen) for the food that they need.

Also, together with the sisters, you must pay attention to the children's shoes so that they do not have such hard shoes that make the feet sore. Where shoemakers are at hand you should have the shoes frequently repaired and greased so that they will be soft. Do not let too many shoes collect, as has happened in some cases and afterward they become too small or are spoiled; do not depend upon the sisters. Also, they shall not order shoes or anything else to be made without your knowledge and consent.

Further, in regard to bed clothing, if a bed has two pairs of sheets, one good one and one not so good, and a child has two nightshirts, that is quite sufficient. But if something more is necessary, you should report it to the manager (*Haushalter*).

Likewise in regard to woollen clothing, whether for boys or girls, for the sisters are especially inclined to dress up the girls for church festivals with dresses and jackets and bodices and afterward lay them away and then they become too small in time and much loss is occasioned. Moths also get into them. For this reason you yourselves should look after the matter, whether for girls' or boys' clothing, and if new clothing is made for the children, you should turn in the old clothing to be used for lining, since it is probably still worth at least a little. Furthermore, in regard to feather beds or comforts which are sent to the school with the children and are worn out or become too small, you should take care that the sisters do not without your knowledge re-cut them and empty them out or make them larger. You should not give in to them in such a matter, but instead should have this done with the counsel of the manager if such alterations seem necessary; and your policy should not be built on the idea, as some are saying, that there should always be a reserve and the school not be completely without such supplies.

Further, you should yourself be with the children when they go to sleep and should be present when they get up, and should yourselves look after the placing of the beds and not rely altogether upon the bedroom maid, so that the children who are clean are kept together and those who are not clean are kept together; likewise, those who have impetigo should be together and the bedding and other things washed separately.

Further, in regard to the children who are not well or where one fears paralysis (*leem*) or the French disease (syphilis?), the bed clothing and night shirts of such should not be mixed with the clothing of the children or washed together with it, but be kept separate. Likewise in the food and drink one cannot be too careful, for there is great danger among so many children.

The same thing is true in regard to washing and bathing; the two should not be mixed. You must take care and watch carefully in bathing and washing that the unclean children are kept separate.

You must take care yourself that the sisters do not make the suds and the water for bathing too hot for the children. You should feel with your own hands whether it is tolerable, and if it is too hot you should forbid the sisters to use it, for it has often been the case that the skin of the children has become as red as a crab and yet they would say: "Why that is not too hot; you are not to bother about such things. But, you must not pay attention to such remarks.

Further, if a child has eczema, you should not let it be bathed or washed so often. It often has happened that although a child reported this ailment, nevertheless it has been compelled to bathe, and it was told: "Oh, that will not hurt you, you bad boy," or "bad girl."

Further, you should not bathe the children every fortnight, for this is not necessary, but bathe them once in four weeks and wash them every fortnight, unless there is a special reason or on account of scalp disorders.

SCHOOL MANAGEMENT CODE TO BE DISCUSSED WITH THE SCHOOL PERSONNEL

This Code, presented below, includes the Code which was formulated during the time of Peter Walpot, except that this Code has been expanded through the addition of many necessary points during the time of Brother Hans Kräl.

P. W. / H. K.

Herein several necessary points are[1] listed as to how the brethren and sisters in charge of the schools, together with their assistants, are to keep order in the training and care of the young.

In the first place, *they must constantly keep in mind why they have been assigned to the children by the Lord and by his people.*

Further, because order in the schools depends largely on the schoolmasters and school-mothers, they shall work together peaceably and trustfully and take advice from one another, and keep a firm and constant order in all the aspects of the care of the young; for quarrelsomeness and laziness create disorder. And the assistants shall also adapt and conduct themselves at all times according to the policies set by those in charge.

The assistants shall see to it that no arguing, difference of opinion or loud talking is heard before the children, but with *peaceful, cheerful, tolerant, and disciplined life and* quiet conduct, they shall inspire the youth likewise to quiet and sober living[2] *and be to them a good example. They should avoid vain and idle words so that the children shall not have an excuse for idle chatter.*

Then the schoolmaster and the sisters shall faithfully and persistently hold the big boys and girls to prayer. And when once or twice a week you talk to the children awhile, the sisters should be present as much as possible, being the ones who by example and pattern of life desire to stimulate them to the fear of God; the sisters shall not be running hither and yon but be mindful of the honour of the Lord and the welfare of the young. *Yet the schoolmaster should not occupy the time of the children with long preaching and with much reading of many scriptures and verses because the children can understand and grasp but little.*

---

1 Throughout this text of the 1578 School Management Code, the italicized sections are additions to the original 1568 School Management Code, material added in 1578 during the time of Hans Kräl. Textual omissions in the 1578 text which had been part of the 1568 Code are noted as footnotes below. At this point, for example, the 1568 text adds the word: "sind" ("are"), which the translator correctly added to the translation in oder to grant a smoother translation.

2 The 1568 text adds here: "Hat aber ye ein schwester etwas wider die ander, so soll es nit vor der jugend, sonder an einem sonderrn ort vertragen werden." ("If one sister ever has anything against another, is shall not be discussed in front of the children but at some other place.")

If one or more children commit a misdemeanour, whether by too much useless chatter or other boldness—and the same is to be done with the girls while spinning—the sisters should not all immediately burst in and punish them,[3] but they should be careful in the fear of God not to be too hasty with them. It[4] has therefore been decided, for better accountability before God and man, that the sisters first report it to the brother in the school or the schoolmaster. If they find that the misdemeanour should be pardoned upon a promise to do better, the sisters shall not oppose the decision. But if it is necessary to punish, it shall be done in a reasonable manner.[5]

When the children begin to chatter,[6] they shall be warned once, twice, or three times, and if one or more pay no attention, those who are known to be guilty should immediately be taken out, *and not a whole group*. Also, such misconduct or shortcomings of the children can often be pardoned with a good conscience before God, especially when they ask for it, and it should be easier for us to be a little too easy than too hard because we see that *even the Lord does not always deal with us adults according to our deserts, but according to grace.*

The big boys are to be punished by the schoolmaster and not by a sister. As to the half-grown boys, if the schoolmaster is not present and a boy acts wilfully and refuses to accept the disciplinary rebuke of the sisters, the schoolmother may in case of necessity apply the rod.

But if it is a big boy, it should be held against him until the schoolmaster returns. Likewise the big girls should be punished by a school-mother and not by a brother. Stealing, lying and other grave sins that take place among boys or girls shall not be dealt with by a sister on her own responsibility, but in school, with the advice and counsel of a brother.

If discipline with the rod is necessary it shall be done in the fear of God, with discernment. In case of knavishness, lying, thieving, and unchaste conduct among the bigger ones, severity shall be used according to desert. This shall not be done secretly or in a corner, but in the presence of all the children, so that they may learn thereby to have fear of wrongdoing.

However, if a brother or sister would be too rough, hasty or angry in disciplining the larger and smaller children, by striking and pushing; hitting the

---

3   The 1568 text adds here: "(wie dann lang her vil geschehen ist)" ("[as has happened often for a long time]").
4   The 1568 text adds here "ist" (has), a word which again has been added to the 1578 translation.
5   The 1568 text adds here: "Auch hat man zu zeiten in schuelen gesehen und erfahren, dz man offt ein gantze zeil oder schar der kinder, darunder man etwa ein geschwätz gehört, herfür genumen und allen nacheinander rueten geben, schuldigen und unschuldigen, welches nit mer geschehen solle, dz die unschuldigen sambt den schuldigen sollen herhalten" ("It has also occasionally been observed and experienced in the schools that a whole row or group of children among whom some talking has been heard has been taken out and all of them, the guilty and the innocent, punished one by one with the rod. This shall not be done any longer.")
6   Instead of "So die kinder ein geschwätz haben," as is in the 1578 text, the 1568 text reads: "Darumb wenn sy also schwätzen."

head, the stomach or the mouth—or attempting to hold shut someone's mouth; or hitting the person in bed with a pillow or cover: such measures shall absolutely not be permitted to occur.

When the shepherds or teamsters complain about a boy, the schoolmaster shall not attempt to discipline hastily, without first investigating the matter, but diligently probe and inquire, so that he will know, in view of the evidence, exactly which means and measure of discipline to use, and will act with discretion.

The children shall be made and accustomed not to fight against the rod but present themselves willingly; then one can always deal with them more gently than if they resist; resistance can not and shall not be tolerated.

A schoolmaster shall let the boys go out together to relieve themselves in the morning and afternoon, and also at noon, and shall himself supervise them. But he should also let them go *out* in between times[7] *to care for their needs*, and not refuse them. For the needs of nature do not yield to law; it is also physically harmful to wait too long. The girls shall be treated in the same way, *and not without due concern*.

It should not be hard for a God-fearing school-mother and her assistants to take counsel with a brother and to ask him when they want to take the children out somewhere and bring them back. Likewise, a schoolmaster *shall have sympathy and cooperation for the sisters and shall yield occasionally in matters that do not interfere with the honour of God and good discipline.*

The bread and meat can and shall be served and distributed to the larger children *by the schoolmaster*, unless he has no time or is away; he may than ask a school-mother or other sister to do it.

If they have something like apples, pears, or the like to distribute among the children, neither shall do it on his own responsibility, but it shall be done with the advice of both at a suitable time.

As to the children's outer clothing, there should not be too much on hand, but as much as necessary should be on hand and kept clean. A brother shall hand out the boy's clothing.

It is the school-mother's duty to keep underclothing in order and to hand it out. As the small children below school age, she may assign it to the sister in charge of the table but not to a girl.

The sisters shall be diligent in putting the children to bed and getting them up mornings and evenings, and shall not depend on the girls to do it, so that they know in person how the children are put into and taken out of bed. But the girls may help them carry the children to and from the beds. The sisters shall also clean and wash the soiled ones themselves.

---

7   The 1568 text adds here: "auffs heüsel" ("to the outhouse").

The girls shall be wakened at five in the morning in winter, to spin; then at six the boys can be wakened, and while they are dressing, washing, and combing, the little children should be taken up, dressed, and washed, so that they are properly dressed for prayer and seated at the table. Then the babies can be promptly taken up, dressed, changed, and when they have stretched and run around a little, one can go about getting their food, and not force it into them the moment they wake up,[8] for it is not natural for them.

At night special care should be taken not to put the children to bed too soon after eating, which is unnatural to them, but always lead them about or let them run about, large as well as small; in winter until about six, but in summer until the sun goes down.

And because especially in summer it is often warm and close in the bedrooms, they should therefore be kept up longer in such warm periods. When it is cool they can be put to bed earlier.

During the night the nurses shall see to it that the children, big and little, are sleeping well and are carefully covered so that they do not chill. One of the nurses or another sister shall help the school-mother look after the children until they fall asleep. No food or snack[9] is to be brought to them in bed except some refreshment or a drink for a sick child. The healthy ones should be allowed to sleep, for it is not good for their health to keep eating day and night. Also, the sleeping children shall not be compelled to get up from a sound sleep,[10] but shall be allowed to sleep. If one has a need, nature will of itself awaken it. In cases where a certain boy or girl has a habit of soiling, these can well be wakened to rid them of their unclean habit with suitable discipline. If one happens to wet the bed unintentionally once or twice, perhaps while dreaming, it should be pardoned upon promise to do better; but if it happens frequently the child may be punished for it.

The nurse likewise shall not begin at once to strike a child if it begins to cry at night, but shall diligently use other methods to quiet it.

Children who have not yet learned to speak shall be promptly changed when they *wet or* soil the bed, and linens and pads should not be too sparingly used; they shall not be punished, because they cannot ask and do not understand. But a nurse shall pay careful attention when one complains by crying or screaming, and take it up and put it on the toilet chair, keeping it well covered so that in its bareness it does not chill.

---

8 The 1568 text adds here: "(wie es denn im alten ordnung zedl auch verboten wird)" ("[which is also forbidden in the earlier Code]").
9 The 1568 text adds the following prefix to the next word: "ge".
10 The 1568 text adds here: "wie denn wol etwa geschehen, das man klain und gross aufftriben und aus dem schlaff bracht, auff die schäffel gezwungen unnd erföret hat on alle notdurft, und mer damit zur unsaubrigkait gewenet. Das soll man aber nit mer thuen." ("as has indeed occasionally been done, getting the big as well as the little children up, rousing them our of their sleep and forcing them to sit on the toilet chair and get chilled; this is not at all necessary and tends rather to form unclean habits. The shall no longer be done.").

When little children, who are beginning to talk, soil their beds it can be overlooked two or three times, and dealt with by speaking about it. If that does not help, they may also as a last resort be punished lightly; they will learn to keep clean.

But with the little children the sisters should be especially careful not to be too severe, but be sympathetic and patient with them because of their simple-mindedness and lack of understanding, as mothers do with their children, for they also desire to train them not to be permitted to have their own way too much, but be gradually directed to the Lord, and when they begin to talk, the caretakers shall always teach them to pray at opportune times.

Brethren[11] and sisters in the schools shall be especially careful and take heed to avoid giving offence by discipline and punishment to brothers and sisters from other places who come to visit the school and observe the children, but should spare them.[12]

The boys and girls shall not be depended upon to take care of the little children either by day or by night, nor to take them up or lay them down, but the adults shall be careful to be present, especially when the children get up, so that no one shall be injured.

The brethren in the schools have already been instructed by the elders not to be wrathful toward the children or strike them on the head, *with the fist or with the rod, nor shall they strike on the bare limb, but with moderation on the proper place. It is necessary to exercise great discretion and discernment in training children, for often, one child can be better trained, corrected, and taught by kind words; with them severity is futile. Another can be managed by gifts. A third, however, learns nothing without severity, and does not accept correction. Therefore the exercise of discipline of children requires the fear of God.*

One should show sympathy to the little ones who have just started attending school and should not undertake all at once to break the self-will, lest injury come therefrom. For the children who are a bit larger one must also exercise very diligent care so that we with you can always have a good conscience.

The bed clothing shall be kept clean and shall be regularly changed, and when the little children get up in the morning a sister, with two or three girls, must always be at hand on the stairway to see that no one falls.

And when *the* children are brought to the school[13] they should be carefully examined[14] and if any one is found to have a contagious disease

---
11 The 1568 text adds here: "die".
12 The 1568 text adds here: "und warten sollen, bis sy hinaus kumen; als denn sollen sie die zucht verrichten, doch mit beschaidenheit" ("and are to wait until they get our; then they shall administer the punishment, but with moderation").
13 The 1568 text adds at this point: "dz mans". The 1578 text rearranges slightly the material of the 1568 text at this point.
14 At this point the 1568 text leaves off the suffix "en" of beschaẇen, and adds the word: "unnd".

Concerning the Upbringing of Children

such as scurvy or the French disease (syphilis?) or paralysis (*lem*), he shall be instantly separated from the rest in sleeping, in eating and drinking, in washing, and everything. Also special brushes and combs shall be used for those having scalp eruptions. Those who have scabies shall be put together and not kept with those who are clean; likewise those who have scalp diseases.

If a child suffers or receives an injury on account of carelessness or anything else, the injury shall not be concealed, but help and counsel shall be sought as soon as possible so that the injury does not become more serious.

Also the school mothers shall *often* and diligently *examine the mouths of the children, and when they*[15] reach into a sore mouth with the fingers, they shall be careful that they do not at once with unwashed fingers reach into a healthy mouth and thereby contaminate it too, but shall always beforehand cleanse the fingers with a clean cloth and water before they examine others. They shall likewise demonstrate to the sisters with them how to examine mouths and cleanse them and cure scurvy, and not withhold *this from* them that others also may be able to attend to such things if they are appointed for it.

Brushing shall not be turned over to the girls.

In the case of diseased scalps and sore mouths the school-mother shall take especial care, in particular about contagious diseases, and shall arrange for a separation in all matters, as in part already stated, as for instance in the matter of beds, washing, eating, drinking, spoons and cups, also in the matter of examining the mouth and sitting on the toilet chair.

Once a week the outer clothing of the children shall be examined for lice; likewise the clothes of outside children when they come to school shall have their heads and clothing examined for lice.

When boys and girls are used outside of school to help in tending the cattle or driving the horses, care shall be taken that they do not pick up lice, for they often absent themselves or hide. Therefore they shall appear twice weekly on brushing day.

One should not let the shoes of the children get too hard so that they cause blisters and the parents may have occasion for complaint. Therefore care should also be taken that the outer clothing and the like is regularly repaired.

The new children whose parents are still on probation shall not immediately be clothed in new clothing, but shall for a time be given the old clothing until their parents have proved themselves worthy members.

The nurses (for sickness) shall diligently stay with the sick children, faithfully care for them, so that no one falls over the side of the bed or on the stairs, and if for

---

15 Instead of "den kindern offt die meüler beschaowen, unnd wenn sie", the 1568 text reads: "wenn sy den kindern die bösen meüler beschawen und" ("when they examine the infected mouths of the children and").

any reason she must leave for awhile, she shall earnestly impress upon the mind of the girl who is helping to take good care of the children; but that she, herself, not be away from them long.

Proper food is to be given faithfully to the children, but they shall not be forced to eat. Drinking shall also be attended to so that drinking is not postponed too long or refused so that the thirst does not become so great that they drink to excess, which is harmful.

For the sick children especially one should be free to ask the cooks for what they need; yet this should be done orderly and not each sister run to the cook on her own account, but with the advice of the school-mother, request what is needed.

When children are sick one should not be too severe with them if they ask for this or that, but should be diligent in waiting upon them in true faithfulness as unto God, in lifting and laying down, in cleaning and washing.

And where there are two schools, one for the small and one for the large, the two shall be conducted as though they were one, and not separately. The sisters in the two schools shall faithfully assist one another in combing and brushing, in bathing and washing, as is necessary. In handing things out in both schools, equality and community shall be observed with the sick and the healthy, with open heart, and without advantage or selfishness.

If the parents desire to take their children out of school, *to be with them*, permission may be given *for a definite time* by a schoolmaster or school-mother *with caution in the fear of God as the circumstances dictate; those in authority shall have a definite understanding as to where the children are taken.*

They shall also take care in supervising the larger children who serve as bread cutter, water carrier, bedroom maid, sweeper, dish washer, children's maid, sick nurse, etc., since they have often been found to be frivolous, underhanded, thieving and lacking the fear of God. Wherefore, the adults shall take diligent care to supervise and watch over them so that no one shall be found blameable for them; such shall not be sent to the beds.

Neither brethren nor sisters shall of themselves undertake or order anything new without the counsel, knowledge, or will of the elders. Even though someone knows a better method, it shall not be followed without good counsel.

When the sisters go out into the field or into the garden with the children, they shall with the utmost care stay with the children so that nothing happens to the children. The schoolmaster shall also be along as much as possible.

The big boys or girls should not by any means be allowed to bump or hit the children or pull their hair.

The sisters shall take special care that the small children are kept clean.

Concerning the Upbringing of Children

More than one sister also shall not often leave the room at one time, to attend to their own affairs, but one shall inform the other.

They shall not carry hot water into the rooms so that no one will be burned.

They shall not bathe the children in too hot water, *for that is harmful.*

They shall not let them sit too long on the toilet chairs lest they take cold or strain too hard.

The washerwoman shall be careful with the fire and in heating water and shall not depend upon the girl who is helping her.

The night nurse shall take good care of the light at night and shall frequently go about among the children to look at them and cover them.

The school-mother shall not arrange matters for the sisters or for the girls without the counsel of the schoolmaster.

If a child murmurs and will not keep quiet in bed, it shall be taken out so that the other children may not become restless, for sometimes one child is itchy, another one thirty, a third has some other need which one does not know. For this reason it is not possible to bring everything to order by using the rod. During the day in school one should not attempt to settle everything with blows, but moderation should be used.

Also, no sister shall show disfavour to a child under her care or any other child, nor show partiality against one that would prefer not to stay with her.

Neither brothers nor sisters shall show favouritism to particular boys or girls or send them to special places, to their beds or other places, for they soon begin to pilfer snacks and become proud.

Likewise the schoolmasters shall not for any reason of their own, for the sake of some business or other cause, ask to be absent from or leave the school without the counsel and consent of the elders. They shall not engage in work outside the school, such as planting or building or repairing and thus neglect their work in the school. They must not by any means go to the markets now and again and buy according to their pleasure, but rather they shall ask for the things they need at the place where these things are provided.

They shall not occupy themselves with writing and reading nor entrust supervision to others who often deal with the children out of favour or disfavour but they shall themselves supervise the children.

The sisters likewise shall not pursue their own interests, in sewing and mending or the like and shall not depend too much upon the girls, nor should they go about too much outside and then when they come into the school, accept a complaint from a boy or girl and then without proper knowledge proceed to deal out punishment. It is therefore our opinion that they should faithfully remain in the school and take care of the children, since by diligence, discipline is often minimized and even unnecessary.

No one shall unwillingly, with complaint or impatience, serve the needy ones of the Lord at this place, for there would be no blessing in such work and the children would in consequence have to pay for it with violence and rudeness in discipline. For where good will is lacking, there are improper words: "You lousy children," etc, "one must be continually occupied with you, one cannot do anything for himself," so that all who hear it would be grieved and the Lord, who hears and sees all, cannot be pleased by such conduct and will call for an account at his time. Therefore each one should willingly and cheerfully strive to please the Lord.

It is therefore the appeal, order, and opinion of us as elders to all of you who have the youth in charge, brothers and sisters, and especially you who are appointed as schoolmasters and school-mothers, that you attend and supervise with all diligence as faithfully as is possible[16] by the grace of God, that this and similar rules of order be observed, heeded, and performed by you and your assistants faithfully and harmoniously so that in these and other necessary points which would be too long to write and possibly also are not necessary, that you may keep a peaceful order in all aspects of your care and supervision of the youth, as those who must give an account for them,[17] that you may do it with joy for the Lord in Heaven, who will also be a faithful rewarder of your diligence.

In conclusion, let each one deal with the children by day and by night as if they were his own, in giving food and drink, taking them up or laying them down, or leading about or carrying, or even cleansing and washing, whatever is necessary, so that each one may be able to give an account before God and may have a conscience void of offence before the godly and the ungodly.

All this, which has been written here and told at some length, is a pattern of how to talk with the school people. At time more should be said and at times less, according to what circumstances require at each place. Each one will know how to adapt himself to it so that the honour of the Lord may be promoted.[18]

The kitchen help and the waiters shall be told that they shall prepare and distribute with good will the food and drink which has been ordered for the children according to their need whether sick or well, young or old, and they shall not make many words about it.

And if it is necessary to ask for some particular food for a sick child, out of the usual order, they shall avoid using rough words. If what is asked for cannot

---

16 Instead of "zum", the 1568 text reads: "auffs".
17 Instead of "darfür," the 1568 text reads: "darumb".
18 A codex in Olomouc, Czechoslovakia, includes an addendum to the main text of the Schulordnung, which was translated by Harold S. Bender, and printed in the *Mennonite Quarterly Review* (see Introduction above). This appendix is included here as a later addendum, probably from the 1600s.

be given, there should be a clear explanation, so that no one give occasion for complain to another.

C[laus] B[raidl]

Anno 1588. Herein follow several points decided upon and discussed with the people in charge of the schools. In addition, the entire School Management Code was read.

Anyone who brings wine to his children in school shall be reported, so that he may account for it.

If anyone brings many gifts for his children, they shall also be shared with the needy and the orphans.

Gifts for the children shall not be given to those outside of school, but only to those in school.

The school staff shall not have the authority to give away to others the things that are given to the children in school.

Concerning giving the children drinks, they shall not single out the children of their own friends to do this, or show preference [in other ways].

They shall not let the beverage stand overnight and offer it the following day when it has lost its flavour, nor give other things only after they have become hard.

They shall not knit caps either for the children or for the adults.

1588

The sister in charge of the beds shall be diligent in her task, keep the floor and bedding clean, so that insects, fleas, or lice do not gain the upper hand and the children would have to suffer much restlessness in bed.

The school-mother shall not rely too much on the bed-keeper, but shall herself see occasionally whether such diligence is exercised. Where negligence is found, each school mother shall have the authority in this matter as well as others to speak about the negligence, and not be silent about it, so that it may be corrected.

No one shall gossip outside the school or complain about the brothers and sisters lest they become distrustful of the school staff.

No distinction shall be made in food out of partiality or respect of persons.

In the school for the little ones they shall keep the children quiet and not permit them to romp and tumble about in the schoolroom or push one another or yell.

They shall not get the food for the big children while the meeting is being held on Sunday, but shall help the big boys and girls to go to the meeting, so that they may also learn to honour the Word of the Lord.

The big boys and girls shall not be permitted to break the bread into the bowls of soup either in the kitchen or in the school; a sister shall do it.

They shall not keep their own hens in the school.

Address delivered in particular to the schoolmasters, January 9, 1596, at Neumühl in the presence of all the elders and stewards.

Since charges have been raised that the children are allowed to be completely disorderly and that in some localities very poor management is used toward them;

Therefore the following points were discussed with them:

Because the school has been entrusted and committed to them by the Lord and by the brotherhood, they shall take faithful heed that the children receive all the care they need in lifting, putting to bed, protecting, nursing when sick, and whatever more is required, so that nothing will be overlooked, but that each child may have all his needs properly supplied.

In addition, with zealous and constant supervision of the children, they shall watch over them and see to it that they do not get into mischief or wickedness or get out of order.

The sisters shall not be left alone with the children; trying to put all the responsibility on the sisters and the nursemaids shall not be practiced. For the nursemaids may report things according to their preference and may be involved in the mischief themselves. If a schoolmaster is with the children in person and keeps circulating among them and quieting them they become more careful and are saved from punishment.

If the children could take care of themselves and had enough reverence for God in them to guard themselves, there would be no need of a schoolmaster.

With severe punishment and long and frequent blows nothing is accomplished.

A schoolmaster shall, whenever possible, seek to avoid punishing them by first warning and reprimanding; if that does no good, use the rod without anger.

Concerning the Upbringing of Children

Everyone shall forgo his personal work, such as sitting at his table to write big books, or involvement with other arts, or long absence from school without good reason.

Whenever one wants to read he shall do it in the morning before the children get up, or at night when they are asleep.

He shall continually and diligently pay close attention to all the children, big and little, but especially to the boys, in and outside the school, so that you may know what is going on.

Since at present the complaint is widely made that too little attention is given the children, that they scatter, run around hither and yon, or that one of them has a way of stealing out of school away from the other children; if anything happened to such a child they would not be able to answer for it if so little attention is paid to them.

Therefore the children shall be carefully watched over; when a boy or girl is missing, immediately inquiry shall be made where they have gone and what they are doing.

None shall be allowed to leave the school without counsel and without permission.

Especial attention should be given in the schoolyard and elsewhere to see that they do not become too scattered and wander away from one another, and that they do not talk or laugh too loudly, or make one another yell.

But they shall be properly quiet when any outside people come to the school so that they may be an honour and satisfaction to the school management and to their parents.

Since children know nothing about good behaviour and propriety, it is necessary to tell them they should not push their way to the table ahead of others, or reach into the dishes meant for other places, and similar things that are unbecoming.

But especially often they should be told to guard themselves from lying and making excuses.

They must avoid wickedness, shameful immorality in bed and everywhere, as well as other evil deeds.

They must not steal or take what does not belong to them. Therefore they shall be diligently taught the Ten Commandments; they should often be reminded of these so that they will learn to know and understand that God loves and blesses the pious, but hates the wicked and will punish them with everlasting fire.

The Ten Commandments can also be written on little tablets and drilled for memorization.

They shall also be acquainted with the Twelve Articles of the Christian faith, so that they will not be ignorant of them.

A schoolmaster shall in general hold the boys to their lessons as much as possible.

He shall listen to charges against the boys, read over their written work, so that the writings of the brotherhood may not have so many errors.

They shall, in addition, seriously reprove their written faults and mistakes, so that they do not form a habit of misspelling and in later life be unable to discard it.

During the boys' free moments, he shall quietly slip to their bedroom area, and where they commonly gather, to hear what their ideas and chatter are about, so that they will always need to remain alert and respectful [in their behaviour].

Also, the schoolmaster is in the school not only for the sake of the children, but also for the sake of the sisters, to be helpful to them with advice, in order that it may best be answerable toward God and man and proceed peacefully and orderly, It is especially necessary to watch the sisters, so that each one will diligently perform her service and not withdraw too much to pursue her own interests.

You and the sisters shall be quiet at your desk, not talking noisily or about things that are not improvable or edifying.

It often happens that a child may get impetigo at school or some other affliction in the eyes or on the hands or feet; if the schoolmaster is spoken to about it, there is often little responsibility shown and one person pushes it off on another.

Therefore the schoolmaster shall keep close watch on the children and have a good knowledge with the others in all necessary matters.

They shall not leave during the time the children are put to bed, and are also to be there when they get up.

Also he shall himself supervise the making of the beds and how they are placed, as well as the children themselves, and not depend only on the bed-nursemaid, to see that those who keep their beds clean are lying together and those who soil their beds are also together; likewise keep those that have impetigo together, and wash their bedding and other things separately.

He should therefore faithfully and frequently look over the dormitories to see how things are going, so that nothing is neglected.

The bedding and night clothes of children who are not well, when there is fear of paralysis (*lem*) or the French disease, or whatever the case may be, shall by no means be put with the clean children's clothing or laundered with them, but it shall be kept separate; likewise with food and drink. One cannot be too diligent; it is necessary among so many children.

The same is true of bathing and washing; here also there shall be no mixing. You yourselves must look after it and faithfully see to it in bathing and washing that the unclean remain separate.

You shall also see to it yourselves that the sisters do not use water or suds that are too hot, and feel it yourself with your hands to see if it is comfortable.

If a child has erysipelas you shall not let it or make it get into the bath and not even wash it.

But a schoolmaster shall be careful to use moderation in dealing with the sisters, not to be too severe with them and think everything should be done his way as if only he understood all things, but, as is stated in the School Management Code, when the honour of God is not at stake he should occasionally yield, be sympathetic and tolerant, because they have to endure much trouble and work and unpleasantness with the children.

It is also included in the School Management Code that when a boy is accused of misconduct, whether by the teamsters or other brethren, the schoolmaster shall not at once proceed to beat him without finding out the facts, but shall give him a careful hearing.

Children should not in anger be beaten about the head with the fist or the rod, nor on their bare legs, but on the proper place.

Besides other charges, not a little information and complaint is brought forward that some take too much liberty in taking the children out of school, and filling them so full of food that they regurgitate it above and below. They are so immoderate that they take them out of school almost every day.

Some take them out of school secretly without permission, so that at times there are few children (such as perhaps the orphans and those who have nobody) left in school.

There is some concern that the school people may at times give the children too much freedom and permit too many to leave the school; but not only that, they even send the children far away across the fields to their parents. They are suspected of doing this not without purpose, but when they can in some way manage to benefit from it.

Others are often given cause [to complain] that liberty is spreading too far and is taking on a carnal, soft quality.

Some have been found who want to put their children to bed and get them up themselves and with cunning reasons are able to get away with walking around with them among the people, which some of them would not have been able to do all their lives in the world. Thus it happens in the brotherhood, without any reticence, that they want to grow back into the flesh, whereas I know that in earlier times they would have been more ashamed of it.

Hens and pigeons and other personal property should be absolutely done away with and all the chickens put back where they belong; they should be used for the common benefit and need.

Likewise, the money received as gifts in the school shall be turned over to the steward, and what needs they have, they shall request from the steward or manager.

A SIXTEENTH-CENTURY HUTTERIAN CATECHISM FOR CHILDREN

God and His Creation

What is God?
God is the only eternal, all-powerful God, the fountain and source of all good, from whom all creatures receive whatever they have that is good.

How is God revealed?
Through everything that he has created.

What did he create?
He created heaven, the earth, the sea, the visible and the invisible, all of it by his Word out of nothing.

Of what did God make mankind?
First, Adam from earth, then Eve from a rib from his side.

To what end did God create man?
That they may know, fear, love, and praise God and live according to his commandment and will, and finally become eternally blessed through him.

What was God's initial will for them?
That they should not eat of nor touch the tree of the knowledge of good and evil in the midst of the garden, for on the day they ate of it they would die.

Where did the first sin come from?
From the devil by his seducing and false advice leading to the disobedience of the first human beings.

What did they do when they became guilty through disobedience?
They ate of the fruit of the forbidden tree, and thereby transgressed God's commandment and fell into his disfavour and thereby brought death and ruin upon themselves and their descendants.

How did that come about?

The treacherous serpent, which was the devil, said to them: You shall not die, but if you eat of it you will know good and evil and become like God. Thus he deceived them.

What did God do to them in consequence of this sin?

He drove them from the pleasant garden of Paradise and into all kinds of trouble and pain, yes, even committed them unto death and eternal ruin.

Were they not able, because of this sin, to find grace again?

Yes, by true repentance and penitence and faith in the promised Descendant of the woman, namely, Jesus Christ, that he would redeem them by the death and sacrifice of his most holy body and blood and reconcile them with the Father.

Does this promised grace not extend also to their children and descendants?

Yes indeed; to all that believe in Jesus Christ, yield to him and are obedient to the gospel of Christ, to them he gives the power to become children of God.

What does this saving grace teach us?

That we shall henceforth no longer live according to our carnal desires and our own will, but live in true piety and righteousness in truth, and serve God with pure hearts.

But how can we become devout and holy?

By love to God and keeping his commandments, also by shunning sin and all that he has forbidden in his Word.

What has the Lord commanded and what has he forbidden?

It is all included and comprehended in the holy Ten Commandments, which the Lord himself wrote on the tables of stone.

Then recite the Ten Commandments to me. The First Commandment:

I am the Lord your God, who brought you out of Egypt, out of the house of bondage. You shall have no other gods before me.

What does the First Commandment teach us?

That in God the Father, Son, and Holy Spirit there are not more than one only, eternal, true, living God.

Can there not also be images in the church of God?

No; neither God nor his saints should be pictured, and all making and honouring of images is forbidden.

What does the Lord require in the Second Commandment?
That we should not take or use his name except for his praise and honour and for the correction, salvation and comfort of our neighbour.

What does the Lord require in the Third Commandment?
That we desist from all sinful works, put them away, and depart from them, and hold still for the Lord to do his works, in order that he may accomplish them in us according to his Word and will to the praise of his holy name.

What does the Lord require in the Fourth Commandment?
That in all external matters we love, honour, fear, and gladly obey our devout parents as well as the servants of the Word of God and our superiors, and also show them all help and sympathy in their old age.

What does the Lord promise children if they hold their parents thus in honour?
That he will bless them here in this life and after this life give them eternal joy and salvation.

What does the Lord require in the Fifth Commandment?
That we shall not be envious, hate-filled, jealous, hostile or angry toward anyone, but in friendliness practice true love, the unity of peace toward everyone.

What does the Lord forbid in the Sixth Commandment?
[He forbids] all evil desires and impulses toward unchastity and impurity of the flesh in thoughts, shameful words and deeds, that we may not become repulsive and abominable to the Lord, but remain pure, holy, and unspotted for him in soul and body.

What does the Lord forbid in the Seventh Commandment?
He forbids not only stealing, but also envy, deception, cheating, wiles, slyness, and all fraud, all of which we are to avoid, so that we may not fall into the wrath of God and be eternally damned.

What does the Lord forbid in the Eighth Commandment?
Not only false witness and testimony, but all evil malice, unjust accusations and judgments, but also backbiting, secret slander and belittling, depriving of honour, gossip, whispering, double-mindedness, and everything that could injure and hurt the neighbour in soul or body.

What does the Lord require in the Ninth and Tenth Commandments?
That we shall guard against the lust of the eye, the lust of the flesh, and against improper desire for anything that has not been apportioned to us. On the

contrary, we shall wish, grant, and do every good thing to everyone, as we ourselves would like to be treated by others.

What does the Lord Christ say of all these Commandments?
He says in Matthew 22: You shall love the Lord your God with all your heart, all your soul, and all your strength and ability, and your neighbour as yourself; and all that you wish people to do to you, you shall also do to them. That is the whole Law and all the Prophets.

Who gives us the power to keep God's commands?
God alone, through Jesus Christ, if we truly believe in him according to his Word.

Concerning Faith

What is the Christian faith?
Faith is a sure confidence in things unseen, which are to be hoped for from God and a clear revelation of his saving grace and a certain attainment of the guarantee and seal of our covenant and of everlasting life.

What is the source of faith?
It comes from the preaching of the living Word of God.

Recite for me the Articles of Faith.
I believe in God, the almighty Father.

Why do you believe in God?
Because he is an all-powerful, abundant whole, and a sufficient condition of infinite goodness.

Why do you call him a Father?
Because he is the true Father, above all that is called father in heaven and on earth, who out of his love supplies and provides all our needs for soul and body, and under his protection he keeps us in our sonship to eternal life.

Why do you call him omnipotent?
Because, in brief, he is, lives, works, and rules over all and in all, whom nothing in heaven or on earth can withstand.

Why do you call him the Creator of heaven and earth?
Because by his eternal Word he created everything, and without it nothing was made; for this reason he is to have that name and also the praise and honour above everything and in everything.

Why do you confess Jesus Christ, the only-begotten Son of God, for God is only one?
Because the Word, which was eternal in God came into this world in this last era and became flesh, for which reason God the Father himself called him his only-begotten Son, Jesus Christ.

What is the meaning of the word "Jesus"?
Redeemer or Saviour.

What is the meaning of the word "Christ"?
The anointed King and High Priest in the spiritual realm and temple of all true believers of his elect.

By whom was the Lord Jesus conceived?
By the Holy Spirit.

Of whom was he born?
Of the holy Virgin Mary.

Who is the Lord Jesus Christ?
He is the Son of the eternal God and of Mary.

What is the Lord Jesus Christ?
He is true God and true man.

From whom did he receive his divinity?
From the almighty God, his Father.

From whom did he receive his humanity?
From Mary, his mother.

Who was it that said he should be called Jesus?
The angel Gabriel, at Nazareth, when he said to Mary: His name shall be called Jesus.

Where was he born?
At Bethlehem in a stable, and there he was laid in a manger.

Who was the first to announce it?
An angel of God, who said to the shepherds in the field: Fear not; for, behold, I bring you tidings of great joy, which shall be to all people. For unto you is born this day in the city of David a Saviour, which is Christ the Lord.

What is the name of the city of David?
Its name in Hebrew is Bethlehem, in German, "brotthausse," ("House of Bread.")

Did the shepherds believe the angel?

Yes, diligently, for they said: Let us go and see what has come to pass, that the Lord has announced to us; they went and found it as the angel had told them.

Why was the Lord born so poor in the stable, wrapped in swaddling clothes and laid in a manger?

Because by his poverty he wanted to detach man from the lust of the flesh and the riches of this world, and make all those who follow him in this age rich in their souls and afterward eternally rich in heaven.

Why do we call Jesus Christ our Lord?

Because he purchased us by his death; therefore we are no longer our own but have committed ourselves to him with soul and body in Christian baptism in obedience to him.

Why did he have to suffer so bitterly, be buried, and die under Pontius Pilate?

Because he wanted to become a perfect sacrifice for our sins by his suffering and death like a patient lamb according to the will of God the Father.

On what did he die?

On the wood of a cross; after he had been crowned with sharp thorns and mercilessly whipped, and in many ways badly smitten, mocked and spat upon; after all this he had to carry his cross out of the city in his great weakness.

Why did he die?

For the sins of Adam and Eve, and also the sins of all of us.

What benefit to us are Christ's suffering and death?

That we have been redeemed from condemnation to eternal death, reconciled to God, his Father, and accepted into eternal life.

What do the death and suffering of Christ teach us?

The daily dying away of sin and ourselves, also patience and comfort in our suffering and tribulations.

Why was he buried?

Because by his death he wanted to testify to the truth of the message of the holy prophets.

What is the significance of his going down to hell?

To show that no one is excluded from this saving grace, but all who grasp and accept it in faith shall be saved.

Was he restored to life?

Yes; on the third day he arose and appeared again alive, first to Mary Magdalene, and later to all his beloved apostles or disciples, ate with them and spoke to them of the kingdom of God and their mission to the entire world.

Why did he come back to life and be resurrected?

For our salvation and righteousness; also to testify that he is Lord over the dead and the living.

Where did he go when he left this world?

In the sight of his disciples he ascended into heaven and sat down at the right hand of the power of God, his all-powerful Father.

Will the Lord Jesus Christ come again?

Yes, on the Judgment Day he will return to judge the living and the dead.

Where will the devout and believing go?

The Lord will take them all into heaven to himself; there they will live with him and his holy angels in all joys forever.

But where will the wicked go?

Into the eternal fire of hell prepared from the foundation of the world for the devil and his angels.

What is the Holy Spirit?

It is the power of God.

What is the Christian church?

An assembly and community of all true believers and the faithful, both in heavenly and temporal gifts and goods.

What do you believe concerning the forgiveness of sins?

I believe that, just as there was no saving of life outside Noah's Ark, there is likewise outside the church and communion of the saints no forgiveness of sins.

When will we arise again?

When the Lord Jesus comes down from heaven on the Judgment Day with all the angels of his power and a flaming sword.

What is eternal life?

An unspeakable joy, which no eye has seen or ear heard, nor has it entered into the human heart, and which God has prepared for those that love him and keep his commandments.

By what means can we acquire these gifts and mercy for eternal life?
Only by faith and earnest prayer to God for a true recognition of our sinful kind and nature to true repentance and reformation of our life and keeping the commands of God.

Concerning Prayer

In what manner shall we pray rightly?
As the Lord Jesus Christ taught us in Matthew 6.

Then repeat the prayer for me.
Our Father, who art in heaven.

Why do you call him Father?
Because he has adopted us in mercy as his children for life in his kingdom and made us partakers of all his possessions.

Why do you say "our"?
Because we are all alike brethren and children of God and should therefore bear the same care and love toward one another.

Why do you say "in heaven"?
Because heaven is his dwelling-place, but we have no abiding city here but are only strangers and pilgrims.

How is the name of God hallowed?
When one sincerely loves him above all else, praises him, and strives to please him, especially for peace and mercy, so that the world may be convinced and caused to repent.

What is the kingdom of God?
Piety, peace and joy in the Holy Spirit, a holy Christian and God-pleasing life, and after this life eternal life.

What is God's will?
That all who believe in Jesus Christ who repudiate all things and follow him in the new birth, shall not be lost, but have everlasting life.

What is the daily bread?
All physical nourishment and whatever is needed for this life, likewise also the food for the soul through God's Word and Spirit.

What are our debts for which we are to ask forgiveness?
They are the shortcomings, mistakes, and errors in intentions, thoughts, words and deeds that occur every day in spite of our efforts and will.

How are we to conduct ourselves toward our neighbour with respect to such errors?
If he is penitent we should bear such things in love toward one another and forgive as the Lord has commanded us and as in Christ he has forgiven us for everything.

Why do we pray about temptations?
Because I am unable to resist them without his divine aid and power.

What are the temptations?
They are all kinds of evil desires and lusts of the flesh, trials from Satan, and the enticements of the world to wickedness.

What is "amen"?
It is a comforting assurance and wish from the depths of the soul toward God that he will surely hear us and grant us what we have asked for with these words in accord with his will.

On Christian Baptism

Have you been baptized?
No, because I am still too young and immature, for the Lord Jesus Christ has not commanded that little children be baptized; only adults and believers who know, fear, and love God and yield themselves in obedience to Christ and his gospel should be baptized.

Since little children are not baptized, can they still be saved?
Yes, for the Lord Christ has bought it for them by his suffering and death, for as he says, "Of such is the kingdom of heaven."

What is true Christian baptism?
The covenant of a good conscience with God, in which we deny ourselves and our own will together with all ungodly life and conduct; on the contrary, we yield, give, and offer ourselves with body and soul up to God in Christ and his holy church, to live no longer in sin with word and will but to live according to the will and Word of God through the power and aid of the Holy Spirit.

Who instituted holy baptism?
Our Lord Jesus Christ himself, when he said to his disciples, "Go out and teach all nations, baptizing them in the name of God the Father, Son, and Holy Spirit."

Why did he command them to baptize with water?
Just as water of Noah's flood, in which all flesh had to perish and drown, is a symbol of Christian baptism, so it signifies true repentance and the dying away of sin and the reformation of our lives and as water cleanses the body and revives the thirsty, so we are renewed, sanctified, made godly, comforted, revived, and made free in our heart and conscience.

What shall those do who are thus baptized?
They shall live according to the teaching of the Lord and his holy apostles in a new godly walk and life and furthermore not sin any more but obey all that the Lord has commanded, as he himself said, "Teach them to observe whatsoever I have commanded you."

On the Lord's Supper

What is the Lord's Supper?
A celebration in loving and blessed commemoration and memorial of the bitter suffering and death of our dear Lord Jesus Christ, a fervent thanksgiving for his costly redemption and pardon of our sin through the sacrifice of his most holy body and blood.

Who instituted the holy Lord's Supper?
Our Lord Jesus Christ. On the night when he was betrayed he took the bread, gave thanks, and broke it and said, "Take, eat. This is my body that is broken for you; this do in remembrance of me." Likewise he took the cup, gave thanks and said, "All drink of it; the wine of the New Testament is in my blood. Do this in remembrance of me. For as often as you eat of this bread and drink of this cup you shall proclaim the Lord's death until he comes."

Why did the Lord institute the Lord's Supper with bread and wine?
Therewith to indicate that just as bread and wine are food and drink for the human body, so also the communion of his body and blood—namely, the spirit and life in all its fullness which he received from God his Father—is the true food and drink of our souls for a holy, godly life, and after this time for the life of his eternal joy and blessedness.

What else did he want to indicate to us with the bread and wine?
That as he indicated to us by the breaking of the bread and pressing of the wine, his bitter death that he suffered for us out of his divine love, just so has he testified to us that we should likewise, for his name's sake and for the sake of divine truth, that we should willingly give ourselves unto suffering and death out of love for him; and how we thereby in this time of community in his suffering likewise shall also in the hereafter share in his honour and glory.

What do we demonstrate toward one another with this breaking of bread?
We explain and testify to each other that as the bread and the wine that we offer one another in the Lord's Supper is united out of many kernels, we also have become one loaf and one body and members one of another in Christ, our Head, and that each member of this Head and the body, his church, has proved himself in all aspects of his godly nature and in purity of heart and unfeigned love and Christian community, and desires to persist therein to the end with the help of God.

On Christian Avoidance

Is it possible for a human being dedicated to God to sin against God anew?
Yes, indeed, if he does not fear God and diligently give heed to his Word.

What shall he do that he may again find grace and find his way back?
Have genuine penitence and sorrow for it, repent and reveal himself to the devout before the Lord, that he may be judged and punished here in this life in order not to be condemned with the world.

Does Christ's church also have the authority to bind and to loose sin?
Yes, for the Lord Christ gave it two keys, one to bind, the other to loose, and said, "What you bind on earth will be bound in heaven, and what you loose on earth will be loosed in heaven."

How shall such a man who finds grace conduct himself after he has been accepted?
He is to walk so much the more carefully and humbly before the devout and before the Lord; then he will be kept faithful in the faith and attain to a blessed end.

On the Training of Children

How shall children conduct themselves that they may be loved by God and be saved?
They shall pray zealously, be pious, God-fearing, and obedient, faithfully keep the Lord's Word and will which they have learned from their youth in the holy Ten Commandments, in the Christian faith, and the Lord's Prayer, and obey them.

What is their duty when they reach the age of understanding?
They shall learn from the preaching of the Word of the Lord to know the Lord Jesus Christ and also themselves and acknowledge their wrongdoing, be

truly sorry and penitent for it, repent, and be baptized in the name of Jesus for the forgiveness of sin, and through the gift of the Holy Spirit desire [to put off] all ungodly life and conduct, also the love of created things of this world with their self-will, and thus establish a covenant with God and all the devout never to sin against God and against the love of the neighbour, but remain faithful and true, also steadfast in the teaching of the Apostles, in the breaking of bread, and in prayer until the end.

Why should such zeal be applied toward children?
Because God himself commanded it so highly and firmly.

How does it benefit the children?
Thereby they know and are taught that there is one God and that He will reward the good and punish the evil. That means pointing youth to the Lord and bringing them up in his fear. The children should be told and taught that piety, righteousness, and all virtue come from God, and all that is evil comes from the devil. For this reason the unrighteous and unholy will go to hell, but the godly and holy to heaven, for the Lord is holy and his heavenly kingdom is also holy.

Is it sufficient for salvation to have committed all this to memory and to be able to recite in an orderly way?
No, for the Lord Christ says, blessed are those who learn, know, and do my Father's will; but those who do not do it will not be saved but be eternally damned and lost.

Whence does one receive all of this and also acquire salvation?
God grants it, Christ earned it, the Holy Spirit performs it, the gospel proclaims it, faith accepts it, good works prove it, baptism and the Lord's Supper confirm it, the Judgment Day gives it.

> *Vergiss es nicht, liebes Herze mein,*
> *Dies täglich deine Übung soll sein:*
> *Lob Gott, sei fleissig, flieh die Sünd,*
> *So kommst du wohl fort, wo Christen sind. Amen.*

> (Forget it not, my dear young heart,
> This shall daily be your part:
> Praise God, work faithfully, from sin do flee,
> And you shall fare well where Christians be. Amen.)

SOURCE: Codex 365, fol, 46v-74r, Státní Vědecká Knihovna, Olomouc, ČSSR.

TWO SERMONS ON BAPTISM AND THE ACCOMPANYING FORMULAE (TAUFREDEN)

[THE FIRST ADDRESS]

To all who have come here to correct their lives, to desist from the sinful life of this world, to learn God's will, to be converted to God, to seek the kingdom of God above all else, and to commit themselves truly to God in the covenant of Christian baptism.

As it is certainly the most important thing that we have to do on this earth, because we know well and thoroughly that we cannot stay on the earth; it is a short time that we have to live here, Our life in this time unexpectedly comes to an end. Today we are well, tomorrow sick, and soon dead and buried. We also know most assuredly that if we die here and our bodies are put away in the ground it is not yet at an end, but we have before us the most serious situation before us; namely, that after this life we must all come forth again and stand before the judgment seat of Jesus Christ, who is coming with flaming fire and with many thousand saints on the great day of his appearing. Yes, if it could be determined when we die here that death is really the end, it is no wonder that many a person would consider it so very unimportant. But no, no! It is not over yet. We must all arise again on the day of reckoning, on the day of visitation, on the day of the final Judgment. As the Scripture says, judgment will come after death when we become alive again. For thus the works of the good and of the bad will be revealed. Therefore the Scripture says: Consider the last things; do not forget, for after death there is no return.

For that reason it is foremost and most necessary that we consider this, weigh it, frequently take it to heart if we want to be wise and not forgetful of our serious situation, and learn to know God, to fear God, which is the beginning of true wisdom, for this is applicable to all people.

For what good is health, what good is honour and favour with the world, what good is money, what good is property if we do not have God's grace and favour. Why do we breathe and what are we if our life is not directed to God and to salvation, if we should not escape eternal damnation and fail to attain to eternal joy, if we should not be living now that we should live eternally afterward, for without that life this life is death.

It is thus essential first of all that each one learn to realize that there is

One almighty God,

who created the heaven of all heavens and what is in it, the earth and all that is in it, the sea and all that is in it, by which creation of heaven, earth, sea, and all that is visible and invisible he proves himself to be the true, almighty God. In this creation we should note that he who made all things is much more powerful and glorious, indeed, more excellent.[1]

He hung the heavens at an enormous height and spread them like a tapestry. The earth's burden and great weight he fastened in the depths, so that it remains so by the Word of his power. He gathered the sea with its flowing waters and set borders for the rushing and course of the waters. In the firmament of heaven he established the rising of the sun in its order, which brought forth the day. He established the shining sphere of the moon, with its waxing and waning, wisely for the comfort of the night. He lit the circuits of the constellations with a varied glow of bright light for the benefit of the night, so that the light surrounds the earth. On the earth he set up high and pointed mountains, cast the valleys into the depths, and levelled off the fields. The innumerable multitude of all kinds of animals he ordered very beneficially for the varied service of mankind. He commanded the trees of the forests to take root and grow for the benefit of human use, which they have done to the present day. He unlocked the veins of the springs and made them flow; they still obey him. Beyond this, for ornamentation, for beauty, and for pleasure to see, he clothed the earth with the many colours of the flowers and with the unspeakably marvellous green plants and their varied fragrance. In the sea he created a great variety of animals, some small, some medium-sized, and some large. He caused the wind to blow and the rain to fall as a storm, not to mention the fullness of the human race. In short: if we look up, if we look down, if we look to the right, if we look to the left, if we look at ourselves and our bodies, and reasoning power he gave us, our thoughts, our speech, hearing, vision, or whatever it may be that moves our limbs and stirs us, we see nothing but his works and remarkable wonders that we have from him alone, and not from ourselves. All of this points us to the almighty God, our Creator and tells us whom we are to acknowledge and keep before our eyes. We see this book of God's creation daily and learn goodness from it. For there is no created thing that does not teach us, present to us and cause us to recognize something good, and point and direct us to God, our Creator.

He is the fountain of all good things, an inexhaustible sea of all kind deeds, God Shadai, who holds our life and our breath in his hand. All that we have, all that we are, and all that we enjoy every day of our lives to this day is

---

1 [Margin addendum:] Here one may introduce the first chapter of Genesis, dealing with the creation of heaven and earth and all creatures, for the recognition of his omnipotence. 1st day: day and night; 2nd day: sky or heaven; 3rd day: earth, sea grass, herbs; 4th day: sun, moon, stars; 5th day: fish, animals, birds; [and the] 6th day: cattle and the creation of man and the planting of the Garden of Eden.

from him alone, from the Father of lights, from the only, eternal, heavenly, highest and best God, who is the life of every living creature. He is the God of all glory, the God of the heavenly hosts, the God of the angels and powers.

He is the God of the spirits, of all flesh, the God of the eternal light and praise, the God of our salvation and comfort, the God of our hope and confidence, whose honour and glory are incomprehensible, who alone has immortality.

All his creations ought to serve him; his praise, his honour and his goodness is beyond expression.

Since everything is from him and comes from him, as he renews his mercies toward us daily as the morning is renewed daily, and gives us cause every day not to forget him, therefore it is God's will that man should consider, understand, perceive and know this. For

God created man for that purpose,

namely, for his divine honour. For when God created every creature on earth, and there was none among them that could know his omnipotence and give him suitable praise; that seemed inadequate for his omnipotence and deity. Therefore, after creating all the rest, God created man on the sixth day. And God the Lord made man of mud of the earth and blew into his face a living breath and thus man became a living soul. And this was still insufficient; God planted a garden in Eden and put the man he had made into it. And God the Lord made all sorts of trees grow up, pleasant to look at and good to eat, so that man might only understand and know how good God's intentions were for him. For that reason he also gave him more intelligence, reason, and feeling, that he might understand God's will, seek him with his whole soul, fear him, cling to him alone, and be obedient to his Word, and find all his hope, all his comfort, joy and bliss and highest treasure in him, seek all his salvation and help in him through Christ, worship him alone, be thankful to him and praise and honour him, and continually lift his spirit to the God who is ever-living from eternity to eternity. To that end we have been created.

As a sign he created man upright with his head toward heaven and did not have it hang to the ground like a hog or any other creature or beast. This was a sign that he should not be minded toward the things of this earth, and shall not have the things of this world for his highest portion, but that he should be minded toward that which is above, like a tree that is rooted in the earth and cannot exist without the earth, but nevertheless stretches its peak upward toward heaven.

Likewise, although we are living in the flesh, we are to raise our hearts, spirits, and souls to God, our Creator, and our thoughts should at all times be centred on the Highest.

For that reason God also told his former people Israel in the Old Testament: Take heed lest ye forget the Lord your God. At another place he says: Hear, Oh Israel, what does the Lord thy God require of thee but to fear God, to walk in his ways, and to love him and to serve the Lord thy God with all thy heart and with all thy soul. To that end man was created and for that reason he received life and breath.

Let us hear the conclusion of all things (says the Scripture): Fear God and keep his commandments, for that is the obligation of every man. For God will bring all the works of man to judgment, whether they are good or bad.

Christ also tells us in the Gospel why we were created and what our duty is. He says: Thou shalt love the Lord thy God with all thy heart, and with all thy soul, and with all thy mind. This is the first and greatest commandment.

And John says in Revelation: I saw an angel flying in the midst of heaven; he had an everlasting gospel to proclaim to those who are seated and dwell on the earth and to all the heathen and races and tongues and peoples. He said with a loud voice: Fear God and give him the glory, and worship him who made heaven and earth and the sea and the fountains of water, for whose sake we are placed here upon this earth.

All created things have remained in their order and fulfil the commands of their Creator. He gave the sun its order to shine only once, and it is continually doing it just as it did at the time of its creation. He commanded the moon once how to wax and wane, and it most zealously remains in this order. He set the course and circuit of the stars, which they are still running with great care to the present day, and with great trembling they obey him who created them in his honour and praise. The birds in the forests also do their part; especially in the spring time and summertime we see how upon waking in the early morning and likewise before they go to sleep they first want for an hour or more to sing so happily with pleasure and joy; they do it to the best of the ability God has given them, to honour their Creator. The lark, when it is about to eat in the morning, first flies high up toward its Creator and praises God as splendidly and vigorously as it ever can. And it often does this also during the day. Yes, the nightingale keeps it up until midnight and does not cease its song of praise all night long. How much more should the human beings, who have attained to the summertime of the age of mercy in Christ, the spiritual May-time, also praise and honour God all our lives. Especially so, since

God created man in his image.

He said, Let us make man in our image, and in the image of God he created him. But it is not that anyone should suppose that God is the image and likeness of our flesh and blood. On the contrary; Christ says: God is a Spirit, namely the Spirit of Truth. Therefore if we are spiritually minded and our thoughts are toward God, we have God's image. Thus, Paul says, to be carnally minded is enmity toward God, but to be spiritually minded is life and peace. For that reason, when God made man from the mud of the earth, he blew the breath of his mouth, the Spirit of his truth upon man, which was to rule, motivate, and thereby be a praise to him who created him.

As long as man now allows the Spirit of truth to rule, guide and lead him into piety, righteousness, blessedness, singleness of mind and purity of heart and spirit, so long he has and bears this image of God and remains in his place and order. But as soon as he no longer lets the Spirit of God, yes, the Spirit of truth, lead him, but makes the Spirit yield because wickedness is gaining the upper hand, and man then lets the flesh rule and overcome him and gives the flesh the advantage with its desires and will, then he has lost God's image. Just as Adam, the first man, also

Forsook the image of God when he fell into sin.

For when God the Lord placed man into Paradise and wanted to see whether he would remain in obedience to God's will, he forbade him the tree of the knowledge and recognition of good and evil which stood in the midst of the garden, so that by this prohibition he should realize that God was Lord over him who was to command and forbid.

But by the slyness and malice of the devil in the form of a serpent he was deceived and seduced, as we read in the book of the creation, that the serpent was slyer than all the beasts of the field. It said to the woman: Yea, did God say you should not eat of all the trees in the garden? The woman answered the serpent: We shall eat of the fruits of the trees in the garden; but of the fruit of the tree in the midst of the garden God said, Do not eat of it; do not touch it, lest you die. Then the serpent said to the woman: You shall by no means die; for God knows that on the day you eat of it your eyes will be opened and you will be like God and know what is good and what is evil. And the woman saw that the tree was good and pleasant to eat from and lovely to look at; because it would also make wise, she broke some off and ate and gave her husband of it, and he ate. Then the eyes of both were opened and they became aware that they were naked.

Thus they were led astray and lost the image of God and the guidance of the Spirit of truth, righteousness, piety and innocence. After the transgression and sin they learned with sorrow of heart that they were deprived and emptied of all the grace of God, knew good and evil, namely, how utterly evil and bad it is to transgress against God's commandment, and on the contrary, how beneficial it is to keep it.

Before this, they were at home with God and they had childlike and full trust in him, like children to their father; but after they had transgressed and obeyed the serpent and yielded to its will they were fearful and terrified.

When they heard the voice of God the Lord, who was walking in the garden, Adam hid and concealed himself with his wife from the face of God among the trees of the garden. But he could not hide. God the Lord called Adam and said to him, Where are you? Adam said, I heard your voice in the garden and was afraid, for I was naked; therefore I hid. And God said: Who told you that? Did you eat of the tree which I forbade you to eat? Then Adam said, The woman you gave me gave me of the tree and I ate.

And so, because of their transgression in forsaking God, they were expelled from God's Paradise into misery, and the sin clung to them always; therefore the wrath of God their Creator came upon them and their descendants. The earth was also cursed on their account.

That is how it still is today. He who lets himself be deceived and motivated or led astray by the devil (who begrudges man's salvation out of his old envy and hatred) to do that which is against God's will against his Word, and against his commandment, abandons the image of God, so that God will or can no longer know him as one of his.

For whoever lets the spirit of lies and untruth, the old serpent, overcome and deceive him to sin, vice, and unrighteousness, he henceforth bears the image of the devil. Yes, he who chooses sin takes upon himself the devil's image. By this they are recognized, as the holy Apostle John says: Thereby we know which are the children of the devil: he who commits sin is of the devil's minting and stripe, or image. Just as one knows a coin by its stamp and picture, and who minted it, so the devil's is recognized by the sin, vice, and ungodly life they are engaged in which God has forbidden, and completely degenerates, so that just as God takes pleasure in all that is good, so they, on the contrary, take pleasure only in all that is evil, which they pursue and perform. God laments through the Prophet when he says, Hear, Oh heavens, give ear, Oh earth, for the Lord is speaking: I have raised and brought up children and they have fallen away from me. An ox knows his master, and a donkey his master's stall. But my people have no understanding. Woe to the sinful people that are dripping with wickedness, a perverse generation, degenerate children. They have forsaken the Lord, angered the Holy One of Israel, and have retreated from him.

Sin is,

however, nothing but forsaking obedience to God, or disobedience. Out of this all other wrongdoing has grown, like twigs, and has taken the upper hand and is still increasing daily.

The Apostle John says: All unrighteousness is sin. But disobedience is the mother of all sins. Samuel, the man of God, also told King Saul: Disobedience is like the sin of witchcraft. It is a bad leaven that sours all the dough, a poison of ruin, a pestilence of the soul, an evil leprosy of the inner man, which separates us from communion with God and all the devout. In brief, it is the fall from God, in which man departs and turns away from the eternal heavenly and only everlasting chief good, away from the perfect to the imperfect, and turns to the creature, to the earthly and temporal, yes, to himself. For the devil has done the same, and his fall and turning away was nothing else than that he did not remain constant in the truth, turned to himself and wanted to be something too, and cast himself away from God.

Sin must be avoided because the devil loves it and delights in it. Man must flee from and hate sin because God hates it and because it separates us from our God, yes, because it is the death of the soul.

The Scriptures say: The mouth that speaks lies destroys the soul. It is the same with other sins and vices; he who commits them also leads himself to eternal ruin and the death of his soul.

If one becomes so inhuman as to kill his own child and becomes guilty of his own flesh and blood, he is considered a great criminal. How then shall he stand before God who commits sin, kills his soul, and becomes guilty of bringing his inner man to eternal death?

We must therefore flee the death of our souls, just as the hare flees from the hounds, the sheep from the wolf, and the birds of the air from traps and nets. In brief, all living creatures flee from death. Then we should certainly not be worse than the unreasoning beast and should flee the most serious of all—the death of our souls, which is sin and wickedness. Thus, man must maintain great watchfulness and care in this matter, so much the more because we know that in all men and children of Adam

Original sin

adheres, and that they have an inborn sinful nature from Adam, as it is written: All the thoughts and imagination of man is evil from his youth up. And David says: In sin I was conceived and in sin my mother bore me. But Paul says clearly: Sin came into the world by one man and has passed into all men. Since it has come upon us through him, it is clear that we inherit it from him, so that we now have, through Adam, our father, the inclination to sin, yes, the besetting sin, that all of us are by nature inclined toward evil and have pleasure in it. This inheritance is shown in all the children of Adam, who are descended from him in the adamic way; it takes over and consumes all that is good and godly in man, so that no man can acquire it again unless he is born anew in Christ Jesus.

Esdras complains of this evil, perverted nature, when he complains: Oh, Adam, what have you done, for in your sinning thus, not only you, but all of us who are descended from you, have fallen?

Paul calls this inheritance the messenger of Satan who buffets his head. At another place he says: I know that in me, that is, in my flesh—Oh, wretched man that I am, who shall deliver me from the body of this death? And John says: He who says he has no sin deceives himself and the truth is not in him.

But this distinction must be made: having sin and committing sin are two different things. It is like fire that lies in the ashes; although it is fire in itself, since it is not flaming it does no damage. Likewise, when cherries or apples begin to blossom, they do not become cherries or apples if the blossoms are broken off. Likewise with our natural sinful inclination: if we kill, subdue, and discard it before its fruit comes, it is not reckoned against those who have been justified through Christ. Likewise, if one is fasting, even if he smells food and desires to eat it, if he does not eat it he is still fasting.

To what extent original sin is harmful

Original sin is, first, the cause of the temporal death of all men who have been brought into life. Because all have inherited this sin, all, young and old, must taste temporal death. And if Christ had not come into this world as our Redeemer, there would have been no hope of further life. But because he has come and has atoned for not only our sins but the sins of all the world, before the time when original sin has not turned into deeds, it leads only to temporal death, but not to spiritual death, so that the Scripture may be fulfilled: Children shall not bear the misdeeds of the fathers; but he who sins shall himself die. But the one who converts the evil inclination and desire into deeds and lets them break out into wickedness this then also becomes the cause of spiritual death.

Thus, all men have died in Adam, departed and fallen away from God and become worthless; there is no fear of God before their eyes. And even though the Holy Scriptures do not say it specifically, we see clearly in the present

Course and life of this world

how all sins, vices, and unrighteousness have so completely gained the upper hand and are increasing. Sin is no longer considered sin, shame is not shame. There is nothing but false truth, false self-control, false honour, false love, false loyalty. The greatest ruin came upon our first parents when they listened to the serpent; thereby Satan deceived them. Likewise, the devil, the sworn enemy of our salvation, is still leading all the world astray by means of the offspring of serpents and asps, namely, the false prophets and false clergy, that is, by their false doctrine, which is deceptively contrary to the doctrine of God.

When God has said in his Word that the sinners and the unrighteous shall not inherit the kingdom of God, they say: By no means; you shall never die. God is gracious and merciful; we want a God who desires that all shall be saved. Did God say that?

When God in his Word commands man to desist from sin and no longer touch what is unclean if he wants to be a child of God, they say: By no means. We are poor sinners, we are not able to do what is good; there is always the serpent's advice.

God's Word says: Do not put off your conversion until death. Then they say: If we only do penance and repent at the end. Thus the devil leads them under the ice and behind the light by this deception. Then it happens as the Scripture says: Many perish by the sword, but many more by a false tongue.

Thus the four false prophets misled and deceived King Ahab by the false spirit who took possession of them, when they told him to move into battle; he would be successful, for the Lord would be with him. But he never again returned in peace.

Thus also the Scribes and Pharisees, false clergy and Jewish priests led all the Jewish nation astray, so that they crucified Christ, the Son of God. For this reason Jesus said to them: You generation of vipers, how will you escape the damnation of hell? These people are even today guilty of the ruin of the whole world. For when lying enters the pulpit, the devil has his will and has won the contest.

These false prophets take the most shameful people by the hand, as the prophet says, and caress them to strengthen them so that they the less abstain from their wickedness. They say peace, peace, when there is no peace.

That makes the world audacious, careless, and ungodly. And since such doctrine well suits the flesh and is pleasing to behold, like the forbidden tree, there are many, many who follow them and go astray. Thus, Christ says in the Gospel: Many false prophets will arise and will lead many astray. But to his disciples he says: Beware of those false prophets that come to you in sheep's clothing, but inwardly they are ravening wolves. By their fruits you will know them. They pretend well.

They pretend to be pastors and clergy, but if you pay attention, that they are the most carnal of all, yes, ravening wolves; for when they lead a godly man of true faith to the point that he returns to unchristian living, so that he dishonours God and wallows with the world again in gluttony and drunkenness and other wickedness, they are content, then they let him go as if they had just really converted him.

One must therefore consider their nature and life (which is equal to a thousand witnesses). If one looks at their people (who are also their fruits), whom they have been teaching for many years by their sermons, and sees that there is no improvement at all in their living, but that the longer they teach, the worse both they and their listeners become; the longer, the more ungodly. That is the tree, and there are the ravening wolves.

With the mouth they laud Christ to the heavens, but with their lives and characters they trample him underfoot. Life and character are on their tongues a thousand times, but their mouth gets farther and farther from their heart. If people were by chance living Christian lives in accord with the gospel in Sodom and Gomorrah, then people are now living Christian and evangelical lives.

This is the time of which Christ said, As it was in the days of the Flood and as they lived in the days of Noah, it shall also be in the last days. At present it is a noble practice: he who is a great wine hero, who has a big paunch and can take good swallows, so that not a drop is left in the jug, he is an honest fellow and receives fame and victory.

In short, the whole world in general has become a house of cursing and wicked deeds through and through. It pours out its blasphemies by the thousands. Their mouth is often too small, so that their tongue cannot satisfy their heart by cursing as they would like.

Now, it is certain that if one often lets the devil fly out of one's mouth, he must have him first in his heart, for out of the abundance of the heart the mouth speaks. The devil has the reputation of being a blasphemer, and of being a backbiter and a spirit of blasphemy; he has also achieved in the world that they curse bitterly in the name of God and dishonour it by Christ's wounds, torture, suffering, cross, dead body and sacrament, so that the sun must grow pale to hear it and the heavens lose their colour.

Anyone who had a drop of Christian blood in his veins, would rather bite his tongue than to let such things be heard from his mouth. But with the world it is daily bread, and if they could just as easily get away with theft, robbery, and murder without punishment as they do with cursing and dishonouring God, no one on earth would be sure of his life or property. At present one hears this great evil from young and old, so that it could make the hair of a lover of God stand on end; even the children on the streets who can scarcely talk, curse and blaspheme in a way that would be too much for a man of thirty. They also commit all kinds of roguery and mischief from their youth up. They are extremely well informed in all gambling and card-playing; also in drinking, eating to excess, and dancing they are by no means the last. And even though they are still too young to be able to perform all kinds of knavery, they speak many shameful, indecent, devilish words and sing all kinds of amorous songs.

In brief, with words, with acts and gestures one stimulates the other and they practice with one another from their youth so that it cannot be adequately expressed, intentionally drawing one another into sin by all sorts of evil and offensive examples. As if by a band they draw wickedness to themselves and sin like a cart rope.[2]

What shall one say? The world came to this point by the false prophets and their perverted teaching that it is desperate and despairing of godliness and the will of God and think, even say, it is not possible to keep God's commandments. Such words show that they have no faith. If what they say were true, the entire Holy Scriptures would be useless and shoved under the bench. But in the Gospel Christ says to the youth: "If you would enter into life, keep the commandments," and told him from the Ten Commandments what to do. For to believers who are yielded to God it is well possible. For the world it is impossible to do good, but to serve the devil day and night and to do his will, as one can see, is easily possible for them and they wear themselves out in the ways of evil.

They say we are poor sinners, as if that were an honour to God. No, God has no pleasure in it, but rather in the conversion of sinners. Yes, the angels in heaven rejoice over one sinner who repents. The Apostle Paul says: If we, while we seek to be justified by Christ, are found to be sinners ourselves, we would have nothing but sin from Christ. God forbid. Christians are not baptized to be poor sinners, but to a new life, to deny and die to sin and not to let it reign in our mortal bodies. Romans 6.

The world is led astray by false doctrine, so that they think that if they are only sorry and penitent at their death, like the thief on the cross, their affairs will be in order. No, he who knowingly persists in the wrong, and sins on the chance of grace, will be repaid with severity. The example of the thief on the cross is given to us to improve our lives, rather than to imitate his. He who knows better earlier and does not do it will fare differently. He who at his final end must sigh about himself for his ungodly life, will sigh much more when he has to arise from the dead. Esau also wept and sighed, but he did not come to repentance. The foolish virgins also cried and wept, but it did them no good. Judas, the betrayer, also at the end felt sorrow and penitence and sighed deeply. Thus, it is a great deception.

The world looks at the crowd and often says, what happens to others will also happen to me. Where my father and mother went, there I am going too. What happens to the entire world, let that happen to me too. It is as if they were saying: Let me also fare as the first world fared at the time of the Flood. As the five kingdoms of Sodom and Gomorrah fared, let me fare. No; since we see that other people's homes, their children, and they themselves were burned thereby, let us not say, let me fare like them. These are therefore audacious, deplorable words by people who neglect their welfare and commit their salvation to sleep. If many of them were lying in a fiery oven and one

---

2   Jer. 13:23: "For as easily as an Ethiopian can change his skin and the leopard his spots, so easily can you who have grown accustomed to evil do well." [This quotation is a later addition in a different handwriting.]

of them called to you to come in with them, for there was a big crowd there, no one would have a desire to do so even if his father and mother were there; he would instead retreat and flee with great fear while he was able to flee. We should flee all the more, because it costs the death of the soul.

The world says: We have many mighty and learned men and doctors who are of this opinion; they surely understand it. But Christ says about this: what is high before men is an abomination to God. Korah, Dathan, and Abiram, who set themselves up against God and Moses, were also rich and learned men, and with them 250 captains, the lords of the community and men of fame; they knew Hebrew; but they did not understand it after all, and all of them went down to hell alive.

Herod, Pilate, Annas, Caiaphas, the high priests, Pharisees, Jewish priests, and false spiritual leaders at Jerusalem were also powerful people, had from their youth studied the Law and the Prophets in Hebrew. They were also a great multitude, but they were the less able to know and to believe Christ, and still less to tolerate and suffer him than the common people. They were far more blinded and perverted because of the hatred of the old serpent. But why? For this reason: they feared that they would lose their priestly honour and living. They therefore rejected God beyond Babylon. Paul says of divine wisdom that none of the powerful of this world knew it. So it is still today.

The world lies in such blindness that it says: Is such a big world to be damned and only such a small group be saved? That would be a great pity. It is indeed a pity and greatly to be lamented. But we see that in the Flood only eight souls were preserved, a mere handful of righteous against the whole world—at Sodom and Gomorrah only Lot and his daughters. Similarly, among the six times one hundred thousand called out of Egypt only two reached the Promised Land. Esdras says in his book: I have already said and say it now and will say it in the future, that there are many more who will be damned than will be saved—as the river is greater than the droplet.

Christ says in the Gospel of the narrow way that leads to eternal life, that few will find it. Christ says that only the fourth fell on good soil and bore fruit. At another place he says many are called but few are chosen. But that all may see still better that the life and conduct of the world is absolutely against God's commands and that it is not a Christian life, but has deviated far, far from the way of truth, we have in the Ten Commandments sufficient evidence, for God says: "I am the Lord your God. You shall have no other Gods before me." And he says, "no likeness, neither of that which is in heaven nor on earth; do not honour and serve them." Thus, the world is turning it upside down and doing the opposite: much idolatry of wooden, stone, silver and golden likenesses, pictures, saints, patrons and crucifixes; these they honour, bend the knee before them, and fall down and worship them. They do this even though the Holy Scripture condemns it and says: Those who love these things are worthy of death, also those that put their hope in the things they make and honour.

Those who do not have outward idols of wood, stone, and silver have their idols and images in their hearts and in a safe; namely, money, possessions, and wealth, to which they dedicate more love than to Christ, and for that reason cannot partake of the Lord's Supper. Of these idolaters Christ says in the Gospel: He who loves father or mother more than me is not worthy of me; he who loves his sons or daughters more than me is not worthy of me; yes, he who loves anything more than me is not worthy of me. Covetousness is idolatry, says Paul. "You shall not name the name of your God lightly." But one commonly hears everywhere, with old and young, men and women, who use the holiest, most precious name of God so lightly, so vainly, uselessly and shamefully, that in some it has to be every third or fourth word, to affirm every disorderly thing by God and by dishonouring the name of God. This is a terribly horrifying misuse of the holy name of God and is the exact opposite of the Ten Commandments. Under the Law such a man was killed and stoned to death; now they pretend to be Christians. So deeply is the world caught in blindness and deception.

You shall keep the Sabbath or holy day holy. But the course, life, and conduct of the world is the very opposite. For all sins, roguery, pride, villainy, dancing, gambling, adultery, gluttony, drunkenness and all kinds of wantonness and depravity for which they do not find time or opportunity during the week, those they commit on Sunday. Afterward they say: We are to keep the Sabbath holy. If that is keeping it holy, black can well be called white. But still they claim to be Christians; let each decide for himself if it is not a shame and an evil that such people bear the name of Christ.

You shall honour your father and mother. How that is generally practiced one can unfortunately see well, especially God, who is the true Father over all, but is least of all honoured as he should be; he says by the Prophet: If I am your Father, where is the honour you give me?

You shall not kill. That means: do not become guilty of any man's blood, for such a man will not be preserved, says the Scripture, though he flee to the pit. And the holy Apostle John says: We know that a murderer does not have eternal life in him. So the world turns it diametrically around. When they have a murderer in prison, when they take him out to punishment and the wheel, the priests go with him and say he will be in Paradise today, a child of life eternal, whereas that is contrary to the Word of God and the Ten Commandments. Well, they say, he confessed it and he is sorry that he committed such a bad deed. Yes, with torture, pain, and burning they forced him to confess; otherwise he might not have done it. And he is much sorrier that he was caught and cannot commit more murders. They put him on the wheel for the very reason that they were afraid he would do it again. And yet they call him a Christian and comfort him with salvation. Alas, the Egyptian darkness and Babylonian confusion!

You shall not commit adultery. That is the commandment of our God; for this vice is an accursed, damned, and banned abomination that bears eternal death within it. It has gained the upper hand in this world, although it boasts of being Christian. And what is most terrible: those who ought to punish this crime, among them it is most prevalent. Yes, those who claim to be clergy and have vowed perpetual chastity and purity to God, those very men have the rope of whores (which is akin to adultery) about their necks. They cannot take a wife throughout their lives, but they keep house daily with whores. Then they say: Do not act according to my deeds but according to my words; as if they were saying: you have been deceived, for we are rascals and rogues. If that is what the priests do, why should not their hearers do the same?

You shall not steal. That is, do not covet what is not yours. But now it is the custom and practice of this world that everyone deprives the other of his possessions, whether by unfaithfulness, by treachery, by usury or by force; he who can take more does so. All of this is the result of the teaching of the false prophets, the very men who, when a known thief is taken to the gallows, accompany him and promise him salvation and eternal life, all of it contrary to the Word of God and the Ten Commandments, and contrary to the Holy Scriptures. Yes, they say, covering it with this little hat: he is sorry and penitent, whereas he is much sorrier that he was caught so that he could no longer steal. And they hang him for the very reason that they fear he would steal more. Nevertheless, by their false teaching they say he is saved. If that is not the broad way, where one can be saved by murder and stealing, one cannot imagine how there could be a broader way to damnation.

You shall not bear false witness. But with the world it is its daily bread to lie, deceive, and bear false witness. They say a white lie does not matter. Thus it has come about that no one's truth is accepted unless he confirms it by swearing and with an oath.

You shall not covet your neighbour's goods, or his wife, or maid, or anything that is his. The world is given over to such desires, and not only desiring and coveting, but carrying out the desire as far as possible.

Christ taught his disciples to pray the Lord's Prayer. But now when anyone raises his hands to pray and thank God for food and drink, as is his duty, to the whole world, when they see it, it is nothing but a reason for mockery and laughter. The adults are ashamed to pray, but they are not ashamed to curse. They make little children pray who do not understand; they have to do it if it is to be done at all. (John 8. The Jews also said we have God as our Father;

but Jesus said: If God were your Father you would love me. Romans 8. Those whom the Spirit of God drives are God's children.)

They say, "Our Father." But God says: They are not my children because of their spots and the measure of their sins, since they do not conduct themselves like God's children and do not obey him. He who calls someone his father but is not his child, lies with his first word; how could he then be able to pray the rest truthfully?

They say: Hallowed be your name, when they, after all, dishonour the name of God, desecrate and despise it in word and deed, and dishonour his great, precious name. That does not fit together by any means.

They say: Your kingdom come, but the kingdom of this world is much dearer to them; it is much more their aim by day and night. The riches of this world are far more important to them. They do not devote one twentieth as much zeal, care, effort and industry to the kingdom of God as to the temporal.[3]

They pray: Your will be done. They say this in words, and afterward everyone follows his own will according to his own head, however it seems good to him. And there is nothing so tedious, dismaying, obnoxious and bitter as when God prevents and breaks their will, while God's will is performed. (1 Thess. 4. Paul tells there what God's will is. It is the will of God that no man be lost. Ezekiel 18; 1 Pet. 2c.)

They pray: Our daily bread give us today; and when God gives it to them it is no longer "ours." Then it becomes "mine" and "yours" as property, and there is no true community. (1 Tim. 6: Be content with food and clothing. They are not content with daily bread, but carry on usury, they are completely yielded to covetousness. 1 Tim. 6.)

They pray: Forgive us our debts as we forgive our debtors. Their mouth says this, but their life denies it. For if one receives a blow he would rather give three in return; he grants nothing and leaves nothing unretaliated, to say nothing of their wishes and curses upon each other. If one or another of these sicknesses and plagues were fastened on anyone's neck he would not go very far any more. If God would not forgive or pardon one in a different way, many a man would fare badly. Therefore such a prayer is the equivalent of saying: as I have done to my neighbour, so may God do to me too; such a man would be felling his own verdict. (Deliver us from evil. 1 Tim. 6 says, Covetousness is the root of all evil. 1 John 5 says: The whole world lies in evil.)

---

3   [In margin:] Matthew 7: Not all who say "Lord, Lord" shall enter the kingdom of heaven.
    Paul says the kingdom of God is righteousness and peace and joy in the Holy Spirit. But the world says they cannot be righteous; it is not possible for them. But Mary said, All things are possible to him who believes. It therefore follows that the world has no faith, neither can they pray.

They say they believe in God the Father, Creator of heaven and earth, and in Jesus Christ, his only-begotten Son, our Lord. But in their works they deny it. They live as if they were saying in their hearts: There is no God who will punish them for their unrighteous life. And the Apostle Paul does not believe that those have the right faith who do not lead a Christian life and deny it in their works. (Romans 10: For if one believes from the heart, one becomes righteous and his life is reformed.)

They say they believe that Christ is coming to judge the quick and the dead, but they live as if there were no Judgment, as if they did not have to give an account on that day, as if there were no urgency.

They say they believe in one holy Christian church. But they do not know where the Christian church is. Most of them think it is the pile of stones with the high point. Some, because they are blind as children at night and cannot see, say it is invisible and cannot be pointed out with a finger.

They say they believe in one communion of the saints. But in their church there is nothing but selfishness and private possession. And the saints are paintings on the walls.

With their mouth they believe in a resurrection of the body. But their living looks as if they were not expecting a resurrection. (That you reflect on this and follow the will of God as faithfully as possible is what I have wanted to teach you with this admonition. May the Lord our God in heaven, who does not will that any should perish, grant his grace to this end; that is my wish for all of you through Jesus Christ. Amen.) From all this it is clear how the world has fallen so far away from the true faith, from real Christianity, from the way of salvation, and departed into all unrighteousness. For this reason

God's wrath, curse, punishment, and judgment

will come upon the world and will not fail, as little as in the first world. Yes, no one who persists in such unrighteous living can be saved.

For God said to Cain: If you do well you will be accepted, but if you do not do the right, your sin lies at your door. It is as if he were saying: Whether you go out or come back, you will always find it. If you die your sins will follow you. (For their transgression is on their bones. And when you are resurrected, they will also arise with you and be your accuser before God's throne on that day.)

If you refuse to listen to the voice of your God, all these curses will come upon you and strike you, and you will be cursed in your field and on your meadows. You will be cursed whenever you go out; as if he were saying: The wrath of God will continually hover over you. (Woe unto you, ungodly men!

When you are born you are born to a curse, and when you die a curse will be your portion. Isaiah 30 [:14].)

The ungodly must be turned into hell; all the heathen who forget God, to the place where the rich man went. (Isaiah 2: They shall go into the holes of the rocks.) For the Apostle Paul says: The unrighteous shall not inherit the kingdom of God, neither fornicators, nor those who honour images, nor adulterers, nor effeminate, nor abusers of themselves with mankind, nor thieves, nor the covetous, nor drunkards, nor revilers, nor extortioners shall inherit the kingdom of God.

Elsewhere the Apostle says: The works of the flesh are manifest; they are these: adultery, fornication, uncleanness, lasciviousness, honour of images, witchcraft, hatred, strife, jealousy, wrath, reviling, dissension, divisions, enmity, murder, drunkenness, gluttony and the like. Of these I told you before and tell you in advance: those that do these things shall not inherit the kingdom of God.

But the portion of the timid and unbelievers and evildoers and murderers and fornicators and magicians and idolaters and all liars will be in the pool that burns with fire and sulphur, which is the second death, whose smoke arises from everlasting to everlasting; they will have no rest by day or night. There will be weeping and gnashing of teeth in utmost darkness, as Christ himself says (Esdras 9): Those will receive mercy who follow my way.

Some may think this is a hard saying. Yes, it is a hard saying to the sinners and impenitent who persist in their wrongdoing. But their hearts are even harder who hear and know this but still do not desist and reform and refuse to change. For the Word of the Lord will not fail; heaven and earth would sooner have to collapse. (2 Pet. 2: For if God did not spare the angels who sinned…)

But all this is said in order that the person who is concerned with his salvation will recognize that he must begin to believe aright and begin to become a real Christian. (Isaiah 9c: For all who admit to the people that it is well with them are seducers. Isaiah 1: Those who have forsaken the Lord—the transgressors and evildoers—must perish together.)

Therefore, my beloved people, let each one take heed to this that he may escape the curse and punishment of God and on the Last Day find rest and comfort with the children of regeneration, who have walked in obedience to God; for he who does not begin it and consider it here will surely be filled with misery later, and have to weep over himself in great pain; may God preserve us from this eternally. This I wanted to admonish you in my simplicity. May God the Almighty grant his grace upon it.

BEGINNING OR INTRODUCTION TO THE SECOND ADDRESS

Therefore, as you heard above, God the Almighty has always hated and sometimes even punished them and thereby given an example for those who would in the future be ungodly, how he will at the End-time on the Judgment Day punish all the ungodly who do not repent. 2 Thess. 1b, as heard, Romans 2. St. Paul also teaches us, Hebrews 2a, and says about this: We should therefore give more heed to what we hear that we may not let something slip away. For if the word that is spoken by angels is established and every transgression and disobedience has received its just recompense, how shall we escape if we disregard such salvation which was spoken by the Lord after it had begun and is confirmed upon us by those who heard by the witness of God with signs and wonders and diverse powers.

SECOND ADDRESS

The Apostle Paul says: See, now is the convenient time, this is the day of salvation when we can still be helped. Now is the time of grace. After this time another time will come, namely, the day of visitation, the time of punishment and judgment. Now God is calling through his Word: Today, today, if you hear his voice, harden not your hearts. But later comes a time when people who refuse to hear today will call and cry for grace, when God will no longer hear. Zach. 7b; Eze. 8d. Now is the time of summer and of sowing; and what we sow now we will reap later.

Now the door is open. After this time it will be very different; namely, the door will be shut. We have an example of this in the Gospel in the Foolish Virgins. (Hebrews 12d. Let us not neglect God's grace.) Now Christ is still our Mediator, Saviour, Redeemer and Reconciler.

After this time he will be the just Judge and the Punisher of all who have not followed him here, who were disobedient to the gospel. (2 Thess. 1) Hebrews 12: lest anyone neglect God's grace.

Anyone whose sins oppress and drive him, who wants to save his soul from everlasting ruin, from everlasting death, punishment and judgment, who wants to be released from the devil's snares, must begin with true repentance and sorrow for his sins. But he who is to come to true repentance must first

Acknowledge his sins

and acknowledge how evil, wicked, harmful, ruinous and damnable they are. For if a sick man does not realize his ailments and a wounded man his injuries, how would he seek a physician? Only his pain can impel him; there is no other motive. For if a blind man believed that he saw well, a cripple thought he could run well, a mute boasted of talking well, a leper announced that he was clean, and a dying man said he was in good health, such sick persons could not be helped nor counselled; even having a desperate illness, they accept no medicine. So it is with those who do not acknowledge their wrongdoing, do not believe that they are in so bad a condition; Jesus did not come for their sake, as he says: Those who are well need no physician.

Sin is the falling away from God. Sin separates us from our God. It separates us from the kingdom of God. He who commits sin is of the devil. The Scripture says: The mouth that speaks lies kills the soul. It is the same with other sins and vices: he who allows them to overcome him is leading himself to the eternal death of his soul. Now it is certain that if one becomes guilty of his own flesh and blood or kills his own child, that man is considered the most terrible criminal, which he indeed is. Similarly he who sins and thereby kills his soul is a great criminal in the sight of God the Lord and in his own sight; he becomes guilty of his inner man by leading it to eternal death. (Mephibosheth, Saul's son, said to David: All my father's house was naught but people of death before my Lord the King. 2 Sam. 19e. To the church at Sardis the Lord gave the message: You have the name of living and are dead. Rev. 3a. Matt. 23.)

He who recognizes sin properly knows how evil and sinful it is; yes, eternal death, knows what injury goes with it. From this follow

Repentance and sorrow for sin

so that man acquires a hostility, displeasure and disgust for sin and has a real anger with himself for obeying sin and the devil so long, allowed sin to control him and lead him away from God and his truth. This sorrow and penitence is, however, not like that of the world, who say today: I repent and am sorry for my sins, and tomorrow they commit them again. When they have cursed and dishonoured the precious name of God, as the last word they say (if it turns out well): God, forgive it. That is a repentance like that of the man who killed his brother, who with the final blow says: Forgive me now, until I do it again. So it is with the world's penitence; it does not bring mercy from God, nor is it genuine repentance. But he who repents of his sin, and is worried, saddened, and anxious (as he should be) must henceforth more zealously and earnestly guard himself against them, and avoid and flee them as a snake. For that is the effect, power, sign and fruit of repentance. As people say: The burned man fears the fire, and that which has once fallen will not easily be led to fall again. Much more we must flee and hate sin.

The people of this world flee death when a pestilence comes and reigns with its poison at some place; they flee from there and are exceedingly careful not to become poisoned. Much more should we flee and avoid sin, which brings eternal death. For certainly, he who has once correctly realized and repented of his sin would henceforth rather die (as many devout people have done) than willingly and knowingly consent to sin in a single word, to say nothing of deeds, but he will rather all his life feel sorrow and grief for the sins he committed (whereby he incurred the wrath of God, his Creator) if he has become a true lover of God.

They alone will be preserved from the ruin of the world. As God says in the Prophets: Go out and mark with a *tau* the foreheads of all those who sigh and mourn for all the sins and abominations that have been done. Thereafter no one else shall be spared. Those who do not sigh and have sorrow and mourning, who do not have the sign *tau* on their foreheads shall be slain and perish. Therefore Christ also says in the Gospel: Blessed are they who mourn, for they shall be comforted. But he who does not have sorrow for his sins here will be sorry for them there. He who laughs about them here will forever weep blood over them there. Where there is true penitence and sorrow, it will bring

True repentance and reformation,

that is, a true humility and mourning before God, when the heart weeps because of its sins and transgressions. For repenting means humbling and humiliating oneself before God, acknowledging the debt and being ashamed before him for his wickedness. This shame brings a true turn about, so that the man cries and asks God for forgiveness and mercy, and begins on himself to compel, kill and tame his body, break its wantonness and take the reins. For not repeating the offence is the genuine fruit of repentance.

For acknowledged sin worries the conscience and gives it no peace. But the restless conscience seeks, inquires and asks how it can find counsel and salvation. As David says: I lifted my eyes up to the hills from whence my help would come; but my help comes from the Lord, who made heaven and earth. With him every penitent heart finds rest and comfort, as it is written: Whom shall I regard except him who is of a broken and contrite spirit?

An example of real repentance that is valid before God we have in King David. When he had sinned and the Lord showed it and presented it to him through his prophet so that it would be revealed to him, he said: I have sinned against the Lord, and fell into great sorrow of heart and lamented: My iniquities have risen over my head; like a heavy burden they have become too heavy for me. He fasted, went in and lay on the ground all night. The elders of his house tried to raise him up from the ground. But he would not, nor did he eat. Not until the seventh day did he arise and eat. Thus, God showed him grace. It remained a sadness throughout his life. He never forgot it. He keeps lamenting it in the Psalms and asks: Do not remember the sin of my youth and wipe out my transgression.

We also see the fruit of true repentance and reformation in the city of Nineveh, how God sent them his prophet Jonah, had him show them the sinfulness of their lives and to cry out over them the cry that God commanded him; namely, that their wickedness had come before the Lord, and in forty days they would perish. The prophet did this and cried out over the great city of Nineveh. The people of Nineveh believed God, were terrified and frightened by the Lord's call, repented, proclaimed a fast, and put on sackcloth from the greatest to the least. And when the matter came before the king, he arose from his royal throne, took off his robe, and sat down upon the ground. He issued an edict over Nineveh: Neither man nor beast, herd nor flock shall taste or eat anything, nor drink any water; people and beasts shall cover themselves with sacks and unceasingly cry to God; every man shall turn from his wicked way and any evil he was planning; without doubt God will again be gracious and turn from his wrath, so that we will not perish.

Then God saw their repentance and their deeds, that they turned from their wicked ways and were converted and he abandoned the punishment and misfortune that he had planned and did not do it. Yes, these Ninevites repented so earnestly, that Christ says in the Gospel: The people of Nineveh will rise up on the Judgment Day and condemn this generation, for they repented after Jonah's preaching.

Another example of true and genuine repentance is seen in Mary Magdalene, who was a sinner. When she heard that Jesus had gone into the house of a Pharisee, she brought a vial of ointment and stooped to his feet and wept and began to wet his feet with tears and dry them with the hair of her head, and kissed his feet and anointed them. She did not know how she could move him sufficiently to mercy. Thus she received God's mercy, as Christ says: Many sins have been forgiven her; therefore she also loved much.

Also the Prodigal Son, who wasted his possessions with feasting and fast living; when he then fell into misery and poverty, into hunger and worry, he acknowledged his sin and thought within himself and said: I will get up and go to my father and say: Father, I have sinned before heaven and before you. Then his father was gracious and pitied him upon his earnest confession, repentance and return.

Likewise, the publican in the temple gives us an example of true repentance and humility. He stood in a far corner, dared not lift his eyes toward heaven, and said: God, be merciful to me, a sinner. He went home justified. Thus it is today. He whose sins oppress him thus and who comes into the temple of his brethren with such a penitent heart will receive justification from his sins.

For the crying voice of John the Baptist, the preacher of repentance, is still in the wilderness and vale of misery of this world; namely, the voice of the Word of God which prepared the way for the Lord Christ to mankind and cries: Bring forth the genuine fruits of repentance, as if he is wanting to say: insincere repentance will not be valid. For the axe is already laid at the root of the trees. The tree that does not bring forth good fruit will be cut down and cast into the fire. This is certainly not said of the trees of the field, but applies to us human beings.

In the Gospel Christ also cries, Repent! Repent! The kingdom of heaven is at hand. Yes, he calls and says: Come to me, all that are heavy-laden; I will revive you. Take my yoke upon you, for it is light and small, and you will find rest for your souls.

His Apostles do the same, as Paul said to the Athenians, Acts 17: God disregarded the time of their ignorance. But now he commands all men everywhere to repent, because he has set a day on which he will judge the circle of the earth with righteousness.

As God also says through the Prophet: As I live, I have no pleasure in the death of a sinner, but rather that he repent and live. Turn, turn from your evil ways. Alas, why do you want to die? Turn unto me, says the Lord, then I will also turn unto you.

God is still calling in this manner through his servants that he has chosen for himself from the world to be his witnesses that those who now hear his voice and his Word and obey it and come to him

Through faith

he will not reject, but they will find grace. Christ said to the captain in the Gospel: Go your way; as you have believed it shall be done for you. And to the believing paralyzed man: Be confident, my son, your sins are forgiven. And to the sick believing woman he said: Be confident, my daughter, your faith has helped you. And to the Canaanite woman he said: Oh, woman, your faith is great! Be it done unto you as you have believed.

For he came into this world to save sinners as he says: This is the will of the Father: he who sees or knows the Son and believes in him will not be lost, but have eternal life. But true faith is of such a nature, power and fruit that it brings about the leaving off of sin. As Paul says: If you believe with your whole heart you will become righteous. That is the sign of true faith, for true faith is nothing else than attaching the heart to God—that man attaches his heart to God as to the only, holy, heavenly, eternal, very best, and perfect good—that henceforth his confidence and hope is set on him. This is a choice gift given by God to the repentant and is not given to everyone.

For just as unbelief is the heart's falling away from God, so the true, living faith is the attachment of the heart and spirit to God, which then breaks forth in the entire life, like the branches from a tree, and becomes active through love.

Faith is the soul's medicine and the mother of all good things. Without faith it is impossible for anyone to please him. And he who would come to God must believe that he is God and will be the rewarder of those that seek him.

This faith is not a dead, or empty, or powerless, or fruitless faith that lies only on the tongue like foam on water. No, it is something else; namely, if he who believes the gospel does what he believes, he has true faith. Just as there cannot be a stairway without steps, neither can there be faith without Christian fruits. For even though two logs are laid down, it is still not a stairway unless there are steps. Likewise, that is not true faith which is without Christian virtue and evidence.

This is the power and fruit of faith, that one is faithful and believing toward God. Thus, through active, evident and fruit-bearing true faith one is

Grafted and incorporated into Christ

and one enters into his Sonship; as John says: To as many as received him, to them he gave the power to become the children of God, namely, to those who believed on his name. Thereby a person becomes one of Christ's sheep, who is the chief shepherd and bishop of our souls. Thereby man becomes a branch and shoot of the vine of Christ, as he says: He who abides in me bears much fruit; that is, if he is grafted on it. For how can a vine bear Muscatel grapes if it is not on Muscatel stock? Previously we were of the vine of Sodom and the fields of Gomorrah, and bore their fruit; but now we should bear fruit like that of Christ's vine.

Thus man comes into friendship with God, as it is said of Abraham that he was found to be a friend of God.

Then man becomes qualified for the marriage feast and the Lord's Supper, of which it is written: Blessed are those who are called to the supper of the Lamb.

Thus man is pruned and grafted into the good olive tree. Thus we become members of the body of the Lord Jesus Christ, where he is the head and we the members. Thus man becomes a fellow citizen of the saints and a member of the house of God. As Paul says: Our citizenship is in heaven, from whence we await the Lord and Saviour Jesus Christ. Thus the heathen become fellow heirs, fellow-members and fellow-partakers in all the promises in Christ. As Paul says, He has drawn us into the kingdom of his dear Son.

Thus, man enters into union with God, and God with him. And he becomes a partaker of the divine nature; namely thus: As Christ came from heaven, not to do his will, but his Father's will, we should now also strive to do his will.

As he is a prince and king of peace, so also his people should strive for peace with everybody; as he is holy, so also they should strive for holiness and purity of heart. As he is the light of the world, so his people are also among this undisciplined, perverse generation.

Such people are partakers of his nature and life, and are truly grafted to and incorporated in Christ and attached to him. As he is merciful, they should also be merciful.

They then become

Assured, sealed and empowered by his Spirit,

that is, with the Spirit of the promise which God made through the mouth of his holy prophets when he said: I will give you a new heart and a new spirit. That is to say, man will have a different spirit, a different intention, a different desire, a different joy—yes, henceforth a right zeal, pleasure and love for the good, for piety and for that which pleases God. Previously these things were boredom to him.

In the Gospel Christ calls this being endued with power from above, because man then has the power and strength to do what is good and right and stop doing wrong, which he could not stop before.

He is called living water because he waters the garden of God and makes it flourishing and fruitful. He is the sap of the true vine, without which the branches cannot produce fruit.

At another place in the Gospel, Christ calls this Spirit of assurance the Comforter, because then the believer is comforted in all suffering, in the dungeon and in prison, and even in his death.

That is the oil which the Wise Virgins have in their lamps, lest their lights go out; the anointing which teaches us all manner of things, of which Paul says, He who does not have the spirit of Christ is not his. But they who are driven by the Spirit of God are his children. Elsewhere he says, It is God that has established us with you and has anointed and sealed us and given the pledge of his Spirit in our hearts.

This Spirit assures our spirit that we are God's children. Elsewhere the Apostle calls him the pledge of our inheritance.

As long as we allow this Spirit to rule, lead and guide us, we are sure of our inheritance. But when he departs from man because evil is taking the upper hand in him, man has lost the assurance and pledge of his inheritance and sits down between two chairs. God will not acknowledge him on that Day as an heir to his kingdom. For example; if one does not have the pledge that was given he will not receive penny or pound of the promised inheritance; the opposite will happen: he will now be charged with losing the pledge.

Such a man's position will then be like that of one who shows the note and guarantee, but the seal was torn off. Such a man will receive only mockery and injury.

This assurance and seal of the promise of God is offered to mankind in Christ Jesus through the

Gospel,

which is a joyful message of our salvation, which announces peace to us and the immeasurable riches of Christ, which gospel is a power of God that saves all those who believe it. Rom. 1.

This gospel and good message was promised to Adam and Eve, our first parents, after the Fall, when the Lord said to the serpent: I will put enmity between you and the woman, between your seed and her seed. He shall crush your head with his heel. What message and announcement would be more joyful than that the enemy's head will be crushed; that is, its power will be taken away.

It is the joyful message that God gave Abraham when he said: In your seed shall all the nations of the earth be happy and blessed.

The Prophet Isaiah, representing Christ, says: The Lord has anointed and sent me to proclaim good tidings to the poor, to bind the wounded hearts, proclaim liberty to the captives, open the prison doors for the chained; yes, to proclaim the pleasant year of the Lord. What more joyful message is there for a bound man than release and freedom? No more pleasant message could be brought; so also is the preaching of Christ, the gospel of Jesus Christ, the Son of God, which God had promised beforehand through his prophets in the Holy Scriptures and bestowed on us. With what great joy it was announced to the shepherds in the field, when the angel said: Fear not, for I bring you tidings of great joy, which shall be to all people. For unto you is born this day the Saviour, Christ the Lord, in the city of David, which even the angels rejoiced to see. And immediately there was a multitude of the heavenly hosts who said: Glory be to God on high, peace on earth, and goodwill toward men.

By accepting this gospel and grace man enters into the covenant of the

New Testament,

of which God spoke beforehand through the Prophet Jeremiah: The days are coming, says God, when I will make a new covenant with the house of Israel. But not according to the old covenant that I made with their fathers, when I took their hand and led them out of the land of Egypt, because they would not remain in my covenant. But this will be my covenant that I will make with them after those days. I will plant my law in their inward members and write it into their hands, that henceforth none will say to his brother: I know the Lord, but they will all know me, from the least to the greatest, says the Lord. For I will pardon their transgressions and not remember their sins against them. This the Lord said, who gave the sun as a light for the day, and the moon and stars for the night.

When he says: They shall all know me, he indicates that the New Testament is a testament of the knowledge of God, yes of the knowledge of divine truth and of his will. For Christ says: I praise you, Father, Lord of heaven and earth, that you have hidden this from the wise and prudent and have revealed it to infants and children. Yes, Father, it was pleasing in your sight.

When he says: I will remember their sins no more, he indicates that it is a testament of grace because in it our sins are forgiven without the merit of our works, out of nothing but his love and faithfulness, through his gracious merit—the many sins that we committed in our unbelief are forgiven through the sacrifice of his body by the blood of the eternal Covenant, in whom we have redemption. Not by the blood of bulls and goats (as in the Old Testament), but by his bitter suffering, death and the shedding of his blood. Thus, no accounting will be demanded of us for our former debt and sins that were committed in unbelief. Therefore David says: Blessed is the man whose transgressions are forgiven, whose sin is covered. Blessed is the man to whom the Lord does not impute iniquity. Of King Hezekiah we read that when the Lord added fifteen years to his life, he said to God: You have cast all my sin behind your back. How much more should we in the New Testament, to whom God has granted the remaining years of our lives, use the time we have to live to come to correction and repentance; then our former sins are cast behind his back through Christ. The Prophet Micah also says: He will turn again and have mercy on us; he will subdue our iniquities and cast all our sins into the depths of the sea.

It is therefore the content of the New Testament that we take from his fullness, grace upon grace. He is the Lamb of God that takes away the sins of the world for those who let him take them away. But those who persist in sin and do not desist, will still be damned, just as previously.

The New Testament of grace is based on what Christ says to the man who had been sick for thirty-eight years, whom he healed: See, you have been healed. Sin no more, lest something worse befall you. Christ also says to the woman taken in adultery: Go and sin no more; as if he meant to say: lest one thing after another be taken from you, as he told the wicked servant.

The Apostle Peter says: Of this all the Prophets witness, that through his name all who believe in him shall have pardon and remission of sins.

Paul says: God was in Christ and reconciled the world to himself and did not impute their sins to them, and has committed to us the word of reconciliation.

Christ wanted this, his testament and divine will, to reach all nations through his servants and apostles, that they may be invited to the wedding feast and to his Supper. For that purpose he gave them their

Commission

and sent them out for the sake of those who should be saved, and told them: Whoever receives you receives me; whoever hears you hears me. But whoever despises you and despises me despises him who sent me. Elsewhere he says: Father, as you have sent me into the world, so have I sent them into the world. I ask not only for them but for all who believe in me through their word, that they may be sanctified in the truth and be kept in your name.

After his suffering and resurrection he tells them again and commissions them. This command he confirmed again after his ascension, as we see in the chamberer of Queen Candace, to whom he sent the Apostle Phillip when the Spirit said to him: Go to that chariot. When he reached it he preached the gospel to him and baptized him.

It is also seen in Saul, whom the Lord had struck down on the road, and said to him: Saul, Saul, why are you persecuting me? He could well have been able to indicate and reveal his will to Saul and also announce the forgiveness of his sins. But he did not do it, but sent Ananias to him, who told him the will of the Lord. Saul had Ananias baptize him; Ananias announced to him the pardon of his sins, and called upon him the name of the Lord.

The case of Cornelius, the God-fearing captain at Caesarea, was similar: he prayed continually and about the ninth hour he saw clearly in a vision an angel of God come into his room, who said: Cornelius, your prayer has been heard before God. Therefore send to Joppa and summon Peter surnamed Simon; he will tell you what to do. The angel could well have explained to him the will of God and also remission of sins. But he did not do it, and thus did not interfere in his orders; Peter, the Apostle, had to do it. The angel sent him to Cornelius, and he baptized him and raised him up.

Therefore Paul says: We are now ambassadors and bring this message in Christ's stead as though God were admonishing and beseeching you through us: Be reconciled to God, for now is the day of reconciliation.

God deals thus still today, doing his works through his true servants and gathering to himself his own people, as it is written: Gather my saints to me, who regard my covenant more than sacrifice and are thus called from the sinful life of the world through true

Separation,

as God has always divided and separated the devout from the wicked. In the same way God separated and divided the light from the darkness, the day from the night, also put the heat into one place, which is the sun, and then the cold into one place, which is the Arctic region, so he also wants a separation and parting of his people from those who are not his people.

Thus he called Abraham, the father of all believers, to go out of heathendom and out of an idolatrous life and separate himself. He was obedient to God's call and left his home and fatherland, not knowing where he was going. He offered no excuses: I can serve God here just as well, God is in this country as well as in another. If he had done that, he could not have pleased God.

We find the same in Lot. The angels of God commanded him to leave Sodom and led him out, so that he was not destroyed with the ungodly.

Noah also had to separate himself from the first world, as God commanded him. And he obeyed and entered the ark with his family. Thus he was preserved. If in unbelief he had said: Is the whole world to be destroyed? That would be a pity! God can save me just as well outside the ark. That would have been a great mistake.

Thus God called his people Israel out of Egypt and separated them from Egypt, as David says: When Israel went out of Egypt, the house of Jacob from a strange nation, Judah became his sanctuary and Israel his dominion. If they had not left Egypt at God's command, he would not have considered them his possession.

God also admonishes his people through his servants and prophets to separate themselves and leave Babel. As Isaiah says: Depart, depart! Go out from there, and touch no unclean thing, you that carry the vessels of the Lord.

By the Prophet Zacharias God speaks thus: Up, up, and flee from the northern land, says the Lord; awake, Zion, save yourself, you have long dwelt with the daughter of Babylon. So it shall be today, that the children of God shall separate themselves and go out from present-day Sodom, from present-day Egypt and Babylon. As Paul says: Come out from among them, and touch no unclean thing (says the Lord), and I will receive you and be your Father, and you shall be my sons and daughters, says the Lord Almighty.

Thus, also the angel of God in Revelation cries to us with a mighty voice, saying: She has fallen, she has fallen, Babylon the great, and has become the habitation of devils and the holder of all unclean spirits and hostile birds. Come out from her, my people, so that you will not become partakers of their sins and need to receive some of her plagues; for her sins have reached up to heaven.

It is very risky to handle coals, and not become sooty; it is hard to stand in the rain and not get wet—likewise, if one associates with the world, indeed much more like powder that explodes when it comes close to fire. Also, since man is by nature inclined to sin, he quickly takes on a bad example and enticement (of which the world is full) and is thereby injured. Many a person has often resolved to himself to stop doing this or that because it is a great sin; but indeed, as soon as he returns to society he falls again into the same puddle up over his ears.

Not only are we to go out from the world and its sinful, offensive living, but also from ourselves, namely, that we dismiss our sinful flesh and its evil desire by true

Mortification

of our own will and old worldly habits. For the world is in the human heart. If he does not die to it, the other going-out with the feet does no good. In the Gospel Christ calls it self-denial, and the rejection of one's power over himself. Therefore the Apostle Paul says: How shall we desire to live in sin if we have died to it. We know that our old man is crucified with him, so that the sinful body is destroyed and we no longer serve sin. And also: You reckon yourselves (says Paul) to be dead to sin and now alive unto God through Jesus Christ our Lord.

Elsewhere he says: In Christ Jesus I die daily. We always bear the dying of the Lord Jesus in our body, that also the life of the Lord Jesus may be manifest in our body. Paul admonishes the believing Colossians: Then mortify your members which are on earth: fornication, adultery, uncleanness, lust, evil desires, impurity and covetousness, which is honour and service to idols. To the Galatians he says: I am crucified with Christ. Nevertheless I live; but now not I, but Christ lives in me. For the life I now live in the flesh, I live in the faith of the Son of God, who loved me and gave himself for me.

For it is not enough that we hear that Christ was crucified for us, died and is risen, but we must also be conformed to the image of our Lord Jesus Christ. For if Christ and his work is only outside us and not within us it is of no benefit to us. Unless we also arise in a new life his resurrection does us no good. Concerning this resurrection the Spirit of God says in Revelation: Blessed and holy is he that has part in the first resurrection; on them the second death has no power, but he will become a partaker of the joyful ascension of Christ.

This mortification, dismissal and denial of ourselves and our own will then bring forth in man a true

Yieldedness (*Gelassenheit*).

In the same manner as one who dies physically, even if he had many possessions and houses and land, when he is dead and buried they are no longer his. Likewise, those who die with Christ here and are buried as to the old man, also have no temporal possessions. For like a man who goes on an ocean voyage departs from the land and leaves behind the things that are on the land, so the believers who commit themselves into the true ark of

Noah, into the Lord's boat, must cast aside all temporal, earthly, creaturely, perishable things and become yielded. No longer will a person set his heart on them if he wants to be a true follower and disciple of Christ.

That is the oven of yieldedness, of which Scripture says: Like gold in the fire, men are proved in the oven of yieldedness (Sirach 2:5).

Of the disciples of Christ we read that when they were called by him they forsook father, boat, net and whatever they had and followed him. For Christ says: Blessed are they that are poor in spirit, for theirs is the kingdom of heaven. There he surely means those that allow themselves to be led and governed by the Spirit of God so far that they rid themselves of temporal things and commit themselves to follow him in true yieldedness. If one might say: I cannot leave my possessions like that, for which I worked hard and which I inherited from my parents, then I ask: If the son of a prince or king were to come from another country and say, Don't be sorry about your miserable possessions, follow me and come; I will give you an entire principality or splendid duchy—would you not do it? If one who would do that for the sake of a temporal principality or duchy, why not much more for the sake of the kingdom of heaven, which is a thousand times better because it is promised by Christ, the King of heaven and earth?

Christ says in the Gospel: You cannot serve God and Mammon. Mammon is temporal possessions and ownership. He who would serve God must get rid of temporal property and ownership. And as Christ says it is not possible to serve and cling to both, so no man can truly say it is possible, any more than that one can go in two directions at the same time.

At another place Christ says: The kingdom of heaven is like a treasure buried in the field, which a man found and hid, and for joy sold all his possessions (note: all) and bought the field.

Again, the kingdom of heaven is like a merchant seeking good pearls, and when he found a valuable pearl he sold all (note: again all) that he had and bought it. Thereby Christ teaches us very clearly that he who finds and recognizes divine truth by faith (which is the best treasure of all and most valuable of all pearls) shall yield up his temporal possessions and let the pearl be his treasure. The kingdom of heaven is like that; it does not mean that he can keep what he has or had, as he did before. No.

Christ says to his disciples: anyone who leaves houses or brothers or sisters or father or mother or wife or child or land for my name's sake will receive it a hundredfold and inherit everlasting life.

Of the invited guests who were unable to free themselves or be yielded, the first let his fields hold him back, the second his calves and oxen, the third the wife he had just taken and for that reason could not come, we hear in the

Gospel that the Lord became angry with them and said: I tell you, none of these men shall taste my Supper. Thus, every man among you who does not deny all that he has cannot be my disciple.

Paul also says: I have counted everything as refuse and dung that I may gain Christ, the noble pearl.

Wherever such yieldedness and giving up is found among men, there follows immediately the

Christian community [of goods].

Of this God spoke through the Prophet Isaiah: The Lord will visit the city of Tyre. Her merchandise and her hire shall be sanctified to the Lord, for they shall not be laid back or treasured; but the merchandise of Tyre shall be for the citizens of the Lord (as if to say: for the common good) for food and lodging for the hungry and clothing for the aged.

We clearly have this basis for Christian community: First: Because Christ himself observed community [of possessions] with his disciples. In the Gospel we read that Judas, while he was still a disciple, carried the common purse and carried what was contributed to them. Christ did this as an example to us, that we should follow in his footsteps and thereby taught us that in his church and community each one should not be master of his own purse (as in the world), but the one who is ordained for it by the community.

Second: We hold to it as well, since Christ teaches Christian community not only with his deeds but also in word in the Gospel, namely that communal living is a special kind of love. For when one came to Christ and said: Master, which is the most important commandment? Jesus answered: You shall love the Lord your God with all your heart, with all your soul and with all your mind. This is the first and greatest commandment. The second is like it: You shall love your neighbour as yourself. On these two commandments hang all the Law and the Prophets. But loving the neighbour as oneself cannot be done unless we live in Christian community. He who has possessions cannot love his neighbour as himself, say what he will. But the one who lives in Christian community, who spends his sweat daily for his neighbour's sake as well as his own, who works his limbs tired and stooped for his neighbour's sake as well as his own; yes, he who will also seek his neighbour's welfare and salvation as much as his own, by protecting and watching over him—he loves his neighbour as himself. No one can speak of greater love than this. No one can show his neighbour greater love.

Christ says: Sell all (note: all) that you have and give alms. When he says: all you have, he does not mean half or a part, as the world gives alms, but he means that one's entire capital should be offered for the needs of the community.

Similarly, we see, when a young man came to the Lord and asked what he should do to inherit eternal life, Christ said to him: If you want to be perfect, sell all (see: again all) that you have and give it to the poor (of course, the poor and needy in spirit in the community), and you will have treasure in heaven, and come and follow me. Here he tells and orders the young man very clearly that he should rid himself of his possessions, and in addition he calls it perfection. Therefore it is perfection; whatever people may say, we should not fail to do it unless we want to disregard what is perfect and the teaching of Christ.

Thus, Christ praises the poor widow in the Gospel who gave all her sustenance (see: all her sustenance) to God's treasury, as if to say: That is how I want it to be in my church and community. It is therefore not a commandment of men.

Third: We have it also from this: the first unadulterated apostolic church at Jerusalem, upon whom the Holy Spirit descended visibly, observed true community; it was an institution and work of the Holy Spirit and not a human decision. All of this is more valid for us than a thousand witnesses, for they heard and learned it from their Master, Christ. We read in Acts, second chapter, which says clearly: They remained steadfast in the Apostles' teaching and in community. And all (see: all; not only some) who believed were together and held all things in common. Their goods and possessions they sold, and they divided the proceeds among all according to every man's need.

If these are not enough witnesses for anyone, let him read in Acts 4, where he will find it once more, and even more positive to make it better understood: Those among them that owned houses and land or property sold them and brought the proceeds and laid them at the disciples' feet, and they gave to each what he needed. Those were the alms Christ meant when he said: Sell all that you have and give alms. One sees clearly that it was not human invention.

Fourth: We know that community is the will and teaching of Christ from the fact that in the Gospel Christ strenuously opposed private ownership and spoke against it. He says: Oh, with what difficulty the rich will enter the kingdom of God! It is easier for a camel to go through the eye of a needle than for a rich man to enter the kingdom of God. Does someone want to say this is a hard saying? Yes, it is a hard saying for those who cling to private ownership and self-benefit. But their hearts are much harder still who hear these words from the mouth of the Son of God and disregard them. They have hearts of stone for their salvation.

Christ also gives a parable of the punishment of the rich man who had great possessions and a store laid by and called them his goods. God said to him: You great fool! Your soul will be taken from you this night. And the wicked enemy took him away at midnight. We also read in the Gospel that Christ drove the buyers and sellers and moneychangers and merchants out of the temple with a good whip; one finds nowhere else that Christ dealt so severely as here with the buyers and sellers and merchants. He wanted to make us understand that he absolutely did not want such things in his house in the New Jerusalem.

Besides all these, we see how God punished the greedy and selfish Ananias and his wife terribly with sudden death, even though he had sold his goods and possessions. But he took out some of the money and kept it back, and laid some down at the Apostles' feet. Then Peter said to him: Why did Satan fill your heart to lie to the Holy Spirit, and keep back part of the money for the field? Would it not have remained yours as it was, and would the money from it not have been in your power? You have not lied to men but to God. When Ananias heard these words he fell down and died a sudden death. The same thing happened to his wife, who knew that he had taken out the money. And great fear came upon all who heard it. This should also properly be a fear for us. If, then, community is not necessary, as some say, then Ananias suffered sudden and severe punishment.

Fifth: We know also from the teachings and writings of the apostles that in the house of God there should be community. Paul teaches the believers again and again that they should live together as members of one body. If we consider this, the Apostle could not have given a greater and stronger teaching on Christian community.

He writes thus to the Corinthians when he says: We are all baptized into one body. Why that? Because, just as each of the physical body's members does what it does not only for its own sake, but equally in general for the benefit of the other members, and none forsakes the others as long as the body and life lasts, so it should also be in the church of Christ, that none should withdraw his hand from the others, none should forsake the others, but keep the Christian community as long as one of us lives on earth.

Elsewhere he says: We, who are many, are one loaf and one body. Why that? Because, as many grains of wheat are ground together by the millstones and each gives up its whole capacity to make one loaf, but the grain that remains whole is cast out and thrown away, thus we are to be brought together and united by the millstones of God's Word. He who wants to remain whole and belong to himself in private possessions is worthless, just as in the first apostolic church, concerning which we also read: Of the rest, none dared to join them.

The Apostle Paul writes: Let no one seek his own profit but the other's profit. How is that to be explicated? What else can we understand it to mean, except to be applied to Christian community? For if no one is to seek his own benefit he must seek the benefit of all. If one is to seek another's benefit he must certainly not seek his own possessions.

Thus, all the Apostles teach love for the neighbour, which is the mother of true Christian community.

When John says in his epistle that our fellowship is with the Father and his Son Jesus Christ, he says immediately afterward: If we walk in the light as he is in the light, we have fellowship one with another. That is also communion with the neighbour. Thus, Paul says to the Philippians: If there is any fellowship of the Holy Spirit, then fulfil my joy; and he says, just following: And let each one look not on his own benefit but on the benefit of others. This is community in temporal things. Therefore if we have community in the spiritual and divine realm with one another (namely, in the realm of greatest importance), we ought also to have and keep community with one another in temporal things (namely, in the realm of least importance).

Sixth: That Christian community is not a new invention or human opinion, but belongs to the foundation and cornerstone of the first apostolic church is heard and seen in our Christian confession of faith (which is not new) which contains and includes it. For one confesses in the Twelve Articles of the Christian faith: One holy Christian church and one fellowship of the saints. He who believes this and confesses it in words should also do it in works, in deed and in truth. Otherwise, how can he be a Christian? It would then be empty straw with him and come from a false basis.

Seventh: Thus, the deeds themselves are witnesses. We have experienced it often enough and see with open eyes that those who remain with private ownership, under the deception of wealth, and worry about food among the thorns of the temporal; yes, under the covetousness (which is a root of many evil things) they wear out, suffocate, go to pieces, are ruined, fall away and again become like the world. This has happened and still happens to many people, although they think themselves so strong and competent that they want to own it as if they did not, and consider themselves so clever that they can serve God and Mammon together, as did the rich young man. Therefore it is simply presumption against Christ's Word. It is the same as putting a knife into the hand of a beloved child, to his sorrow, injury and death when he falls on it later. For like beetles in horse manure and worms in wood, so covetousness has its dwelling-place, work and being in private ownership.

On the other hand, the work itself bears witness that Christian community, living together and the assembling of believers is the way that is most perfect, most Christian, most sure, most blessed, and most conformed to the gospel for all lovers and children of God. There one can have greater and the very best opportunity to have and hear the Word of God (which is our best portion here on earth), there one devout member can guard and watch over the other, warn him and address and rebuke him as a brother, give each other good counsel, sympathize with one another, bring up the young in the fear of God, so they do not run on the streets, and cannot see and hear the daily Sodomite, immoral, evil examples and enticements of this world. Those are glorious, blessed and great things that can never be repaid to God with thanks.

The Apostle Paul also reflected on this when he said: We should not forsake our assembling, as is the manner of some, but admonish one another, and that so much the more since you see the Day approaching. Therefore, the more these last times become more dangerous, more deceived, more seductive, and more filled with manifold errors, so much the more necessary than ever becomes the assembling and holding together. If it was necessary and beneficial in the time of the Apostles and also at Antioch, where they assembled in the church a whole year, it is much more necessary and beneficial now. And he who avoids the communal life and meeting of the devout, is not Christ's lamb and will surely fall prey to the wolves. God therefore says through the Prophet: Woe to the shepherds who separate and scatter my herd.

Therefore every believer who wants to be one of the Lord's sheep is obligated, by true

Submission (*Ergebung*)

to join the community of the Lord. First, he must submit to God with all his heart and all his soul, for God does not want divided or half a heart; with God it is "all mine or nothing." We have good examples of this in the Holy Scriptures, especially in the penitent Ruth, the Moabitess, who followed her devout mother-in-law Naomi and absolutely refused to leave her, but said: Where you go, there I will go, where you lodge, there I will lodge, your people shall be my people and your God my God. Where you die, there I will die and be buried. The Lord do this to me, and death must part us. By this good resolution, intention and submission she came out of heathendom into the people of Israel and into David's lineage.

We read also of Ithai, the Gathite, who came to David just when he had to flee out of Jerusalem pursued by his son Absolom. Then David said to Ithai: Turn around and go back to your home. Yesterday you came and today you are risking going with us. Turn around, and may mercy and faithfulness come to your brothers with you. But I am going wherever I can. Ithai answered and said: As truly as God lives and as truly as my lord the King lives, at whatever place my lord the King lives, whether for life or death, there I, your servant, will also be and will be found with you. When David heard his final decision, intention and complete submission he said: Come then and go with us. Thus, man should submit and commit himself even today to the true spiritual David.

The Prophet speaks of this submission to the Lord when he says: One will say, I am the Lord's; the second will call on him under the name of Jacob; the third will with his own hand subscribe himself to the Lord and win under the name of Israel.

The Apostle Paul says: Submit yourselves to God as those who have been brought from death into life and your members as instruments of righteousness. In like manner, on the other hand, no more is required to go to hell than that a man freely give himself to the devil as his possession and under his sceptre. That teacher will then lead and master him (like a rider who has his horse under spurs) into doing his pleasure. But on the contrary, a believer should submit and commit himself to the Lord with the attitude that he wants to be to the Lord as the right hand is to the man.

Then the submission should extend to the community of God with all that one has and can be. As Paul says of the church in Macedonia: They gave themselves first to the Lord and then to us by the will of the Lord. Such submission as was also found in the first apostolic church should still be practiced today, namely, that a believer submit himself to

Obedience

to God and his community and let himself be governed henceforth by God's Word and his community, concerning which Christ teaches in the Lord's Prayer that we should pray: Thy will be done. The Apostle also speaks of this when he says: We have received grace and apostleship for obedience to the faith for his name, that no one shall any longer do what he wishes, whatever he desires or concerns him, according to his own mind and will, for that would not be obedience to the faith or obedience to the truth. No, Paul says something different about it: You are not your own, for you are bought with a price.

Just as a human slave is not his own, to do or leave as he wishes, but what his master and his master's officials demand of him, so also we are servants and handmaidens of God, the servants of God in his house. For if we have submitted and committed ourselves to God and his community (as is reasonable and Christian) into obedience we owe it to God with our utmost zeal and earnestness; and that so much the more because we know that what we do from now on, we do not do for men but because we thereby serve the Lord Christ himself, who said: What you do for the least of these among my people, you have done it for me. From him we shall also receive the recompense of the inheritance. Henceforth our labour is not in vain in the Lord.

But he who manages, lives and acts according to his own will and mind is not submitted to the Lord.

Then he who believes, acknowledges and understands this, that is the true entry

To the true Christian baptism,[4]

which Christ commanded and instituted; namely, that one should first be taught and instructed. For as the establishment and institution by Christ says, when he speaks to his apostles and disciples: Go out and teach all nations and baptize them in the name of the Father, the Son, and the Holy Spirit, and teach them to observe all that I have commanded you. There one sees clearly that teaching should precede baptism. And he who baptizes anyone before he has taught him or can teach him does not baptize in the name of God but contrary to God's name and command. For infants know nothing of the name of God, the Son or the Holy Spirit. He says they should be taught to keep all that he has commanded us. That gives the baptism power, and by it we remain in the way and in the will of God. For if we do not observe what he has commanded, baptism is powerless, let one be baptized as he will. It is therefore not child's work.

Christ says, Go out into the entire world and preach the gospel to every creature. He who believes and is baptized will be saved; but he who does not believe will be damned. It is as if he wanted to say, he who does not believe will not be saved, even though he is baptized. Here it says again: first teach, then believe, and thirdly, baptize. One cannot teach infants. Therefore they cannot believe, and hence do not yet need baptism. Infant baptism is the opposite, turning the matter hind-foremost, hitching the wagon in front of the horse. They baptize first and teach many years later and may not believe any more.

Such a man shoots off his gun and later asks where the target is. They set someone up who is supposed to believe in the child's stead. It is as if one were to eat for another; the other would no doubt starve.

John 3: Christ says: Unless one is born again of water and Spirit, he cannot enter the kingdom of God. It is through God's Word that one is born again, for him who understands it, who believes it, who is converted and becomes another being. As Christ says elsewhere to his disciples: Unless you turn and become like little children you cannot enter the kingdom of heaven. That is the new birth. Paul also says: Put off according to the former walk the old man and be renewed in the spirit of your mind, and put on the new man, who is created after God; to this belongs receiving water baptism, the sign of the new covenant, in which one submits himself to God and denies the

---

4 [Margin addendum:] Which is a righteousness it behooves us to fulfil. Matt. 3.

world, sin, the devil and all his being. For this comes the power and giving of the Holy Spirit which God gives; otherwise it is in vain.

Infant baptism is no new birth, but a premature birth; for the water does not give a rebirth to anyone, and baptism is of no value to anyone before he understands it. It does not at all refer to children, for Nicodemus was not a child, but a ruler of the Pharisees and a teacher, but was still unable to understand; then how can infants understand it? They cannot possibly walk before their legs are developed.

Acts 2: When they asked: Men, dear brethren, what shall we do to be saved? the Apostle Peter said: Repent, and each one be baptized in the name of the Lord for the forgiveness of sins. Therefore to those who repent baptism is pertinent. Infants have as yet no need of repentance, therefore none of them needs baptism. What do infants know about it? They would let themselves be baptized in the name of the Turks or of the Pope, in the name of Herod or of Pilate; it means nothing to them.

Romans 6: Do you not know that all of us who are baptized into Jesus Christ are baptized into his death? And as Christ was raised from the dead, so we should also walk in a new life. Then to him who does not walk in a new Christian life baptism is powerless and in vain. Infants cannot walk in a new life; they are still growing day by day into the old life.

Galatians 3: As many of you as have been baptized have put on Christ. That is certainly spoken to believers. Infants know nothing of Christ as yet. What have infants put on? How can infants do anything before they can leave it undone? Infants know nothing at all. They are baptized without their knowledge, without their will and desire, whether they wish it or not. They have to submit to baptism; whether they laugh or cry, it must be done.

That is not true Christian baptism by far; it is not Christ's command but against Christ's command, against the teaching of the Apostles, against the practice of the Apostles. Who can honestly and truthfully show that anyone should be baptized against his will?

Ephesians 5: He gave himself up for us that he might sanctify us, and cleansed us by the washing of water by the Word. Now, we all know that water does not cleanse anyone's inner being, but you are clean, says Christ, because of the Word. It is therefore not a washing with water in the Word because the word is spoken, but because the hearer believes the word, because teaching goes before and with baptism and falls or is received into the heart. Infant baptism is not a washing with water in the Word, because teaching and the Word cannot be used with infants.

Titus 3: According to his great mercy he saved us by the bath of regeneration and renewing of the Holy Spirit. Why is Christian baptism called a bath of regeneration? Because it belongs only to those who are born again through the Word of truth. For no one can be reborn without God's Word. There is no renewal by the Holy Spirit outside the Word of God. Children are children and remain children until they mature. They are not renewed or changed.

1 Peter 3: Baptism is not putting off the filth of the flesh, but the sure knowledge of a good conscience with God. Baptism does not take away the evil, sinful nature and being in our flesh, but reminds man to strive against it and not to let self reign, but to strive to enter into it with a pure heart and a good conscience. Herein I exercise myself that I may have a good conscience void of offence toward God and all men. From this it follows that if one's walk is not with a good conscience, there baptism does not have its power and is like a letter without a seal. That is also against the baptism of infants, for they know nothing of a good conscience toward God.

These and many other Scriptures we have on true Christian baptism. But about infant baptism there is not one word in the whole Bible; it is therefore wrong and against God. And since it is not something good, nothing good comes from it, but it gets worse and worse. They claim that children must be damned and deprived of God's face if they die unbaptized. There they seriously interfere with God's judgment. For infants are by no means to be damned while they do not know right from left nor good from bad and are still in innocence. It would have been a thousand times better for many an adult if he had died in childhood without baptism that to suppose he is baptized and lives and walks so shamefully contrary to Christ's teaching.

True Christian baptism means something very, very different. And he who makes such a vow to the Lord and obligates his soul should not weaken his word but do all that has proceeded from his mouth, so that he does not become a liar to God his Creator.

Thus, he who has entered into Christian baptism with the Highest and incorporated into the Christian church and fellowship of the saints can afterward observe the

Supper of the Lord

Jesus Christ properly with all the believers, as the Lord instituted it, that we should do it in remembrance of him, so that it may never be forgotten whence have come our salvation and our redemption; namely, through the suffering, death and shed blood of our Lord Jesus Christ. He made the sacrifice for us that is valid through eternity. And as a memorial and a celebration of thanksgiving he instituted the Supper. And thus the Apostles observed it. When the priests and their followers reek of and drip with mischief and sins they try to cleanse and scour themselves with the false priestly sacrament. But people who want to observe the Supper of Christ worthily and observe it as it is revealed in Paul's teaching in 1 Cor. 2, must be clean and unspotted by sin.

Since Christ's disciples did not eat their Lord and Master bodily as he was sitting beside them at the Supper, much less will the priests eat him now that he has ascended on high into heaven.

Even if the soldiers who crucified and killed Christ and treated him so cruelly, had at that time taken him down and eaten him, it would not have helped to forgive their sins. 2 Cor. 6. Christ does not agree with Belial; they cannot dwell together. Mark 5. The evil spirit said to Christ: What have I to do with you? Since, then, it is obvious that Christ and Satan cannot be together, it is also obvious that Judas, the traitor, did not partake and eat of the true body of Christ with the other apostles; for it was after receiving the bite of bread, in other words soon thereafter, that the devil entered into him. If, as the priests believe, he had already eaten the body and blood of Christ when Satan entered into him, then Christ's body and Satan would have been dwelling together in the same house, namely, in Judas.

Also, if at the Supper Christ had given his body to the disciples to eat, where would he later have found the blood, since the body had already been eaten? If he had first taken the blood from his body, the body would have been without blood. Also: in Leviticus there is a strict commandment that the Jews should eat no blood. If Christ had given the disciples blood to drink it would have been against the Law, and the Jews would have considered it a terrible wickedness, as is seen in John 6. Also, it is written: They broke bread from house to house.

This Supper of Christ has been distorted and perverted by the world into serious idolatry and abuse. No one should eat of it unworthily. But they do just the opposite: When they find themselves burdened by sin and may reek and drip with vices, they go to the sacrament and take it for the forgiving of sins. Then they are thought to be clean. No, that is not its meaning. Besides, they give it to murderers, thieves and evildoers, and then hang the thief together with the sacrament on the gallows. If it were the body of Christ (as they assert), they would be hanging the body of Christ on the gallows and giving him his portion with thieves and murderers. But they are counterfeiters, who thus only deceive people, of whom Christ warns us in the Gospel: When they say, here is Christ, or there, we are not to go there and are not to believe it. For nettles cannot produce roses. Also, Christ has only one body, not so many hundreds of thousands of bodies.

They call it the most venerable sacrament, but before one can look up and around it is a most terrible oath and curse for them, and they dishonour God with it so that the earth might tremble. Thus they themselves imprint an evil seal on it so that one can see what kind of a tree it is.

He who thus commits himself in the covenant of Christian baptism takes upon himself the

Cross of Christ.

The Prophet Isaiah speaks of this: The truth is taken captive, and he who removes himself from evil men must be robbed. Elsewhere: They will rob and slay all those who fear God. They will take their goods for themselves and drive them from their homes. Then it will be seen who my elect are. Son, if you desire to enter the service of God, equip yourself for trials. Set your heart and suffer patiently, and if you are arrested, do not evade them.

The cross of Christ is persecution, sorrow, suffering, mockery, shame, and hatred and enmity of this world; as Christ says, Matthew 16: If anyone would follow me, let him take up his cross and follow me. It does not say, as some think, I will not take a cross upon myself. But if one does not know how to take up the cross of Christ, let him only repent and leave off the sinful life of this world and he will already be bearing the cross on his neck. He does not need to worry further about it.[5]

That is how Christ fared. As soon as he was baptized he was tempted by the devil. Similarly today, if one commits himself to the Lord in the covenant of Christian baptism and stops serving the devil and repudiates him, temptation begins at once.

All the lovers of God before us and all the holy prophets and just men fared thus. It did not just begin with us. The Lord Christ himself fared in this manner at the hands of those learned in the Scriptures and the false priests. And thus the Apostles fared, as Christ foretold it to them: You must be hated by all men for my name's sake. Men will persecute you from one city to the next; they will take you before their rulers and into their prisons. If they called the Father Beelzebub, how much more will they do so to his household. They will cast out your name as evil. If the world hates you, know that it hated me before you. If you were of this world, the world would love its own. The time is coming when he who kills you will think he is serving God thereby. We must enter into the kingdom of God through much tribulation. All who want to live God-fearing lives must suffer persecution. Do not fear any of those things that you must suffer. Behold, the devil will cast some of you into prison and you will have trials for ten days. Be faithful unto death and I will give you the crown of life.

Therefore we, who have sought Jesus the Crucified and also found him by God's grace, cannot preach another Christ to anyone, or promise good times and rest. Although the present is a good time, there is no assurance that

---

5 [Margin:] We have to bear a cross here. If we do not want to bear Christ's cross we will have to bear the devil's. Blessed is the man who takes Christ's cross upon himself.

it will last;[6] as our forefathers were often sentenced by fire, water and sword for Christ's sake, for the sake of their faith and for the sake of divine truth. Thus, nothing else is to be expected. For this the believer must equip and adapt himself. We are no longer to return blow for blow, reviling for reviling, insolence for insolence, vengeance for vengeance, but leave it to him who said: Vengeance is mine; I will repay, says the Lord.

That is tight and narrow, but the right and sure way to everlasting life, and he who persists until the end will be saved. He will then have gained it for eternity.

Questions to be asked those who have yielded themselves.

Question: How to recognize of what mind they are?

Which one has debts or other bad dealings? (besides brotherly address and reproof).

Or if one has promised or become implicated with a woman. They should announce it and ask for counsel.

If we should learn of it later on, we would say he made a false submission and did not enter the brotherhood in the right way.

What the church of Christ is and how one is led into it, namely, the real ark of Noah.

As Mary conceived the Lord Christ by faith and the Holy Spirit, and placed her will into God's will, so we too must accept Christ in faith; then he will begin and finish his work in us. That the *Gemeinde* (brotherhood-church) has the key to loose and to bind. Matt. 16.

1. Admonition to weigh the cost, which those who commit themselves to the service of Christ must prepare for temptation, for all who would live godly lives in Christ Jesus, must suffer persecution and the hatred of all the world.
2. He who does not come voluntarily should not be compelled, but must account for himself if the Lord finds him unprepared.
3. No one shall undertake the matter for another, for it is not the work of man or human association; each must build his house on the true rock, Jesus Christ, so that it may last. Matt. 7.
4. Submit to brotherly address and rebuke. These shall be practiced in God's house.
5. No one should any longer have possessions of his own, for he commits and gives himself to the Lord and his church with all that he has and can do.

---

6   This passage gives further documentation as to the dating of the manuscript: most likely pre 1593.

6. That there is no obligation to return a person's goods to him; he should be told this at the very beginning.
7. He who is involved in improper dealings which are punished in the world, or has brazenly become involved with a woman shall first indicate it and receive counsel and not enter the brotherhood, for we could not defend him; he would have to be responsible for himself.

Questions to be asked when baptism is to take place

Have you now understood the Word of the Lord from the instruction and preaching, and do you acknowledge it to be the divine truth and the way to eternal salvation?

Do you desire to give and offer yourself up to God the Lord with body and soul and all that you have, and no longer to live according to your own will but submit yourself to obedience to Christ and his members?

Are you truly sorry for the sins you have committed against God in your ignorance or unbelief, and do you desire henceforth to fear God, never knowingly or willingly sin against God, but rather die than to commit an act against God deliberately and knowingly?

Do you also desire to accept and to bear brotherly address and rebuke, and where necessary also to use it toward others?

Do you also believe that God has shown mercy to you through the death of Jesus Christ and the intercession of the saints and has forgiven and remitted your sins committed in unbelief?

Do you also desire to yield yourself to the Lord, set up a covenant with God and to be baptized upon the confession of your sins?

Answer Yes.

Upon your confessed faith I baptize you in the name of God the Father, Son and Holy Spirit. May the Almighty God, who has shown mercy and grace to you, draw you and fill you with the grace and strength of his Holy Spirit from above. And may he inscribe you into the book of everlasting life and preserve you devout and true until the end. This I wish you through Jesus Christ. Amen.

Arise and sin henceforth no more.

But if anyone sins after knowing the truth and by true repentance and correction confesses that he is penitent, he shall be received again.

Question

Have you cleansed your heart so that you have nothing more upon you but that all has been revealed and brought to light, that might hinder your salvation? —Note well, God is a listener.

Are you sorry from the bottom of your heart for the sins you have committed against God after knowing the truth? And do you confess that you bore the punishment as reasonable?

Do you desire as a result to do right and henceforth fear God?

Never again willingly and knowingly sin against God but rather die than henceforth knowingly act or sin against God?

And do you desire to submit yourself to God anew, give and offer yourself up to him? Also to commit yourself in obedience to Christ and all his members, accept and bear brotherly address and reproof? Also, where necessary apply it to others?

Do you believe that God will give you grace and strength for this? Do you also believe that God the Lord has forgiven and remitted your sins through the death of Jesus Christ and the intercession of the saints?

Answer Yes.

Since God the Lord has given you a penitent heart I lay my hands upon you as a witness and on behalf of the whole Gemeinde. I announce to you in the name of Jesus Christ the forgiveness of your sins. May God the Lord, who has been gracious to you through Christ, inscribe you again into the book of life, grant you grace and strength and keep you devout and faithful until the end through Jesus Christ. Amen.

Arise and sin henceforth no more, lest something worse befall you.

FIRST ADDRESS [AN ALTERNATE VERSION]

All of you who are assembled here to be instructed and taught through the Word of God in the things that might be useful and good and edifying for your welfare and salvation, in order that you may spend the time you have left to live in accord with God's will and invest it well and receive in your hearts an assurance, a true, living hope, be satisfied with God and his people, after having previously spent your lives against God and his Word in all manner of sin, in all unrighteousness, in gluttony, drunkenness, covetousness and all vices when you were led by the false prophets who give men false hopes and proclaim peace where there is no peace.

So much has already been told you from God's Word, that the world with its evil life before repenting and correcting its ways will not stand before God, but retribution and wrath, tribulation and fear will come upon them and upon all the souls of men who do evil. Romans 2.

For that reason some of you have come here, forsaking your homelands and native lands that you might put off your wrong living and follow and be obedient to the teaching and gospel of Christ.

Therefore this day has been appointed that you may be still further taught and instructed what the will of God is; also what the difference is between us and the world and what we learn of God, how he is all-powerful and the only Power; why God created man at the beginning, namely, for his honour; and how God created man in his image and gave him a command which he transgressed; and when he became disobedient, forsook God's image and fell into sin, how God punished him for it; since his descendants also sinned, how God punished them at many different times; concerning this we will tell about the terrible example of the Flood and the expulsion of the Sodomites with fire from heaven—note well how it happened and how God set an example thereby for all those who would in the future be ungodly and persist in their sins irreverently, without repentance. Luke 13a. 1 Pet. 2.

We therefore confess and say that he alone is God, who exists in and of himself, who has neither beginning nor end, to whom all power belongs both in heaven and on earth, for which reason the word "God" belongs to him alone; although there are other gods—that is, those who are called mighty, there is nevertheless only one God and Power over all of them, so much more than all the others that there is no other power outside that which proceeds from him and is given and lent to the others.

How God says through the Prophet Isaiah, Chapter 43: Note that I am he before whom there was no God and that none will come after me. I alone am the Lord and beside me there is no saviour. I warn and I make whole; I teach that you shall take no strange God, and you must bear witness to me, says the Lord, that I am he from the beginning of time, and there is none that will snatch it from my hand, and what I do no man can turn aside.

And further, Isaiah 44. I am the first and the last, and beside me there is no god. For who has there ever been beside me, who exists from eternity; let them name him and reveal it that he may be compared with me. They tell you past and future things, and that without any fear and hesitation. For have I not long ago proclaimed and warned? You must bear witness to me whether there is a God beside me, or also a Creator, whom I do not know. (Deut. 32f.) See now that I am and there is no God beside me. I can kill and make alive; what I have wounded I can heal. And there is no one to save it from my hand.

But that everyone may note and understand why we ascribe solely to God the Lord such great honour, fame, omnipotence, and all power, all glory and majesty; what causes us to do it is this: namely, that with Paul we believe all that is written in the Law of Moses and in the Prophets, and have our trust in God that in the future will be the resurrection of the dead, both righteous and unrighteous. Acts 24.

Second, we see and learn this from his works since the creation of the world, how God performs his works before our eyes, by which we are to recognize the power of the Master-workman. For the wise man (Sap. 13) says: Vain and useless are all people who have no knowledge of God and who have not been able, by the visible good things, to recognize him who exists for himself eternally, and who have not perceived or recognized the Master-workman from the created things.

If we look properly at the created things and God's works we notice how God created the heavens and the earth, all creatures including the human race.

Genesis 1. In the beginning God created heaven and earth, and the earth was desolate and void. And it was dark upon the deeps and the Spirit of God moved upon the water. And God said, Let there be light, and there was light. And God considered the light good. Then God divided the light from the darkness and called the light day and the darkness night. And the evening and the morning became the first day.

Second Day

And God said: Let there be a firmament between the waters, and let that be a separation between the waters. Then God made the firmament and separated the water under the firmament from the water above the firmament. And it happened. And God called the firmament heaven. And the evening and the morning became the second day.

Third Day

And God said: Let the water under heaven gather in separate places, so that one can see dry land. And it happened. And God called the dry land earth and the gathering of the waters he called seas. And God saw that it was good.

And God said: Let the earth bring forth grass and herbs that will seed itself and fruitful trees, each bearing fruit according to its kind and having its own seed within itself on the earth. And it happened thus. And the earth brought forth grass and herbs that seed themselves, each after its own kind; and trees that bore fruit and had their seed within themselves, each according to its kind. And God considered it good. Then the evening and the morning became the third day.

Fourth Day

And God said: Let there be lights on the firmament of the sky and divide day from night and be signs of day and night, days and years, and let there be lights on the firmament of the heaven to illuminate the earth, and it happened thus. And God made two great lights, a large light that ruled the day and a small light that ruled the night, and in addition also the stars. And God set them on the firmament of the sky to shine upon the earth and to rule the day and the night and divide the light from the darkness. And God saw that it was good. Then the evening and the morning became the fourth day.

Fifth Day

And God said: Let the water speak and stir up moving and living creatures and winged fowl that fly under the firmament of heaven. And God created great whales and all kinds of animals that live and move; and the water stirred up each according to its kind. And God considered it good. And God gave them many gifts and said, Be fruitful and multiply and fill the water of the sea, and let the winged fowl multiply on the earth. Then the evening and the morning became the fifth day.

Sixth Day

And God said: Let the earth bring forth living creatures, each after its kind, cattle, creeping things and animals on the earth, each after its kind. And it happened thus. And God created the animals on the earth, each after its kind and cattle after their kind. And saw that it was good.

And God said: Let us make men in our image according to our likeness, who will rule over the fish in the sea and over the birds under the heaven and over the cattle and over all the earth, and over all the creeping things that creep on earth. And he created man in his image, in the image of God he created him, male and female he created them.

And God blessed them richly and said to them: Be fruitful and multiply and fill the earth and bring it under your control, have dominion over it, have dominion over the fish in the sea and over the birds under the heaven and over all animals that creep on earth.

And God said: See, I have given you all kinds of herbs that seed themselves, fish that seed themselves on the whole earth, and all kinds of fruitful trees, and trees that seed themselves, for your food and for all the animals on the earth, and for all the birds under the heaven and for all creeping things that have life and all the green herbs for food. And it happened thus. And God saw all that he had made, and behold, it was all very good. Then the evening and the morning became the sixth day.

Genesis 2

Thus the heaven and the earth were finished with all their hosts. And thus God completed all his works that he had made by the seventh day, and rested on the seventh day from all his works and blessed the seventh day and sanctified it because he had rested on it from all the works that God had created.

And God created man of clay or dust of the earth and blew into his face a living breath. Thus the man became a living soul.

Thus God created man in his image. But no one should think that flesh and blood are the image of God or that flesh and blood are equal to the Godhead. For it is taken from the earth and is earthly. But the image of God is of heaven and is heavenly. Christ says God is a Spirit. John 4. For when God the Lord created man he formed him of clay of the earth. He was then not yet the image of God, but only an earthen vessel, and there was as yet nothing living in him. Then God blew a living breath into his face, and only then did man become a living soul. Thus God the Lord created man in his image.

Thus God the Lord created man solely for his glory; for this purpose he gave him intelligence, reason, and sensibility above all other creatures...

Genesis 3

And the serpent was slyer than all the animals of the field that God had made, and said to the woman: Yea, did God say you shall not eat of all the kinds of trees in the garden? Then the woman said to the serpent: We eat of the fruit of the trees of the garden, but of the fruit of the tree in the midst of the garden God said: Do not eat of it, do not touch it, lest you die. Then the serpent said to the woman: You will never surely die, for God knows that on the day you eat of it your eyes will be open and you will be like God and know what is good and evil.[7] ...woman saw that the tree was good and...to eat some of it, and lovely to...that it was a pleasant tree, since...approached and broke off some of the fruit and...the man of it too, and he ate...eyes of both were opened. And...that they were naked, and...branches and made them skirts...Voice of God the Lord in the garden...in the garden, when the day was cool...Adam hid with his wife...of God the Lord among the...and God the Lord called Adam...are you? and he said, I heard...was afraid, for I am...myself, and he...are naked...might acknowledge his will and zealously strive to keep it, cleave to him alone, seek, love and honour him alone, for that is honour, that man or the creature of his hands remain in the station in which it was created and set down and not be moved from it. Thus, God created man into a heavenly being that he might be heavenly and divinely minded and seek that which is heavenly and divine. Acts 17f.

---

7   Partial text only, due to the mutilated original codex page.

And so man fared well as long as he remained in the image of God, which is holiness, guiltlessness, righteousness, purity.

And God planted a garden in Eden[8]…facing the east and said to the man…that he had made, and God the Lord let…all kinds of trees pleasant to see and good…and the tree of life in the midst of the…the tree of the knowledge of good and…

And God the Lord took the man…into the pleasure-garden of…Eden, which he…God the Lord commanded the man…You shall eat of all kinds… but of the tree of knowledge…evil you shall not eat. For…eat of it you shall surely die…both the man and…and were not ashamed…from the earth, and now, cursed be you of the earth, which opened its mouth and received your brother's blood from your hands. When you cultivate the field it will henceforth not give you its strength; a fugitive and wanderer shall you be on the earth. But Cain said to the Lord: My sin is too great to be forgiven. Behold, you are today driving me out of the country, and I shall hide from your face, and must be a fugitive and wanderer on the earth. It will happen to me that whoever finds me will slay me. But the Lord spoke thus to him: Anyone who slays Cain, on him it shall be avenged sevenfold. And the Lord made a sign on Cain that no one should slay him, whoever might find him. And so Cain left the face of the Lord and lived in the land of Nod on the other side of Eden east of the garden.

Genesis 6

But when men began to multiply on the earth and daughters were born to them, the sons of God looked at the daughters of men, how beautiful they were, and took as wives the ones they wanted. Then the Lord said: My spirit shall not always strive with man, for he is also flesh and his days shall be 120 years. There were at that time also giants or heroes on the earth, for when the sons of God slept with the daughters of men and they bore children to them, they became powerful in the world and very famous people. But when the Lord saw that the wickedness of men was great on the earth and all the imagination and thoughts of their hearts were always very wicked, he repented that he had made men on the earth, and it worried him in his heart. And he said: I shall wipe out from the earth the men I have made, from men down to the cattle and to the creeping things and to the birds under the heaven. For I repent that I made them. But Noah found grace before the Lord.

That is Noah's birth. Noah was a pious and upright man and lived a godly life in his times. There were born to him three sons: Shem, Ham and Japheth. But the earth was corrupt before the eyes of God and full of wickedness. Then God looked on the earth and behold, it was corrupt, for all flesh had corrupted its way on the earth.

---

8   Partial text only, due to the mutilated original codex page.

Then God said to Noah: The end of all flesh has come before me, for the earth is full of their wickedness; and behold, I will destroy them with the earth. Make for yourself an ark of gopher wood and make rooms in it. And pitch it with pitch inside and outside, and make it like this: Three hundred ells in length, fifty ells in width and thirty ells in height. You shall make a window in the top one ell in size. But you shall set the door in the middle of its side, and you shall build the ark with three stories—into the lower and into the middle and into the top storey. For behold, I shall send a downpour of water upon the earth to the destruction of all flesh in which there is the breath of life under the heaven. All flesh shall perish and everything that is on the earth. But with you I shall make a covenant. And you shall go into the ark with your sons, with your wife and with your sons' wives. And you shall put into the ark all kinds of animals, of all kinds of animals a pair of each, male and female, that they remain alive with you, of the birds according to their kind, of cattle according to their kind, and of all kinds of creeping things on the earth according to their kind. Of all of these, one pair of each shall go into the ark with you, that they may remain alive; and you shall take all kinds of food with you that are eaten, and you shall take them with you to be food for you and for them. And Noah did all that God commanded him.

Genesis 7

And the Lord said to Noah: Go into the ark, you and all your family. For I have seen you righteous before me at this time. Of all kinds of clean animals take seven and seven of each, male and female, likewise of the birds under the heaven seven and seven of each, male and female, that seed may remain alive on all the earth. For after seven days I shall send rain upon the earth for forty days and forty nights, and wipe out from the face of the earth all that has life that I have made. And Noah did all that the Lord commanded. But he was 600 years old when the water of the Deluge came upon the earth. And he went into the ark with his sons, his wife and his sons' wives. Before the Deluge there went in with him into the ark of clean animals and of unclean, of the birds and of all creeping things on the earth in pairs, male and female of each, as the Lord had commanded. And when the seven days had passed, a downpour descended upon the earth in the six-hundredth year of Noah's age, on the seventeenth day of the second month, that the fountains of the great deep broke open and all the windows of the heavens opened, and a rain descended upon the earth for forty days and forty nights.

On the same day Noah went into the ark with Shem, Ham and Japheth, his sons, and with his wife and the three wives of his sons, besides all kinds of animals according to their kinds, and all kinds of birds according to their kinds, all that could fly and had wings, all of them went with Noah into the ark in pairs, of all flesh that had living breath, both male and female, went in as God had commanded. And the Lord shut the door behind him.

Then came the Deluge upon the earth for forty days and forty nights, and the water increased and lifted the ark and carried up over the earth. Thus the water prevailed and increased greatly on the earth so that the ark rode upon the water. And the water increased so greatly on the earth that all the high hills under the whole heaven were covered. Fifteen ells deep the water prevailed over the hills, which were covered. Then all flesh perished that crept on the earth, whether birds, cattle, animals, and all that moves upon the earth and all men, all that has living breath on dry land died. Thus everything was wiped out that was on the earth, from men down to the animals and the birds under the heaven; everything was wiped out from the earth. Only Noah remained and what was in the ark with him. And the water stood on the earth 150 days.

When men later again multiplied, they should have learned from the harm suffered by their parents, but the bold flesh was so wicked in its way that they could not grasp the Lord's work, but evil increased and they grew even worse than the first had been. For the bad seed had been sowed in the human heart, as Esdras says, IV Esdras 4: For the bad seed is sowed in the human heart by the evil one. But how much wickedness it has brought forth up to the present time, and how much more will it still bring forth before it reaches the threshing-floor.

Genesis 11

All the world had one tongue and language. As they journeyed toward the east they found a plain in the land of Shinar and went there and said to one another: Let us make bricks and burn them, and they used bricks for stone and pitch for mortar. And they said: Let us build a tower and a city, whose point will reach to heaven, that we may make a name for ourselves before we are scattered into all the lands. Then the Lord came down to see the tower and the city that the sons of men had made. And the Lord said: Behold, they are one kind of people and one language among them all, and they have begun to do this. They will not desist from all they have planned to do. Let us go down and confuse their language there, that none may understand the others' speech.

Thus the Lord scattered them from there into all the lands, and they ceased to build the city. Therefore its name is Babel, because there the Lord confuses the languages of all the nations and scattered them from thence into all the lands.

Genesis 12; 22

Then God chose for himself from all the nations a man called Abraham; he set up with him a covenant of peace, that he would be his God. He would make him great and bless him richly. Now, when Abraham agreed to the covenant, God tempted him with his son Isaac. Genesis 22. But when God discovered his obedience the Lord found pleasure in him and said: How can I hide from Abraham what I am going to do (Genesis 18), since he is to become a great and mighty nation? For I know him well enough to know that he will command his children after him to keep the ways of the Lord and do what is right and just, that the Lord may send upon Abraham what he has promised him.

And the Lord said: There is a report at Sodom and Gomorrah that is serious, and their sins are very grievous. I will therefore go down and see if they have done all that is rumoured that has come before me, or if they have not, that I may know, And the two men turned and went to Sodom. But Abraham stood still before the Lord and drew near to him and said: Will you destroy the righteous with the ungodly? There might perhaps be fifty righteous men in the city. Would you destroy them, and not forgive the city for the sake of the fifty righteous men who might be there? Be it far from you to do that and kill the righteous with the ungodly, that the righteous would be like the ungodly. Be that far from you, who are the Judge of all the world. Should he not judge with justice? The Lord said: If I should find fifty righteous men in the city of Sodom, then I will forgive the city with all its places for their sake. Abraham answered and said: Alas, behold, I have sinned in speaking with the Lord, although I am dust and ashes. There might perhaps be five fewer than fifty righteous men in it. Would you then destroy the entire city for the five? He said: If I find forty-five I will not destroy them.

And he continued to talk to him, and said: Perhaps forty might be found there. But he said: I will do nothing for the sake of the forty. Abraham said: Do not be angry, my Lord, for my speaking more. Perhaps thirty might be found there. But he said: If I find thirty there I will do them no harm.

And he said: Alas, behold, I have sinned in speaking with my Lord. Perhaps twenty can be found there. He answered: I will not destroy it for the sake of the twenty. And he said: Do not be angry, my Lord, that I speak once more. Perhaps ten could be found there. But he said: For ten I will not destroy. And the Lord went his way when he had finished speaking with Abraham, and Abraham went back to his place.

Genesis 19

The two angels came to Sodom in the evening. Lot was sitting in the gate at Sodom and when he saw them he arose to meet them and bowed with his face toward the ground. And he said: I pray you, my lords, turn in into your servant's house and spend the night. Have your feet washed, and get up early tomorrow morning and go on your way. But they said: No, we want to spend the night on the street. Then he urged them strongly. And they went into his house. And he made a feast for them and baked unleavened bread, and they ate it.

But before they retired the men of Sodom came and surrounded the house, young and old, all the people from every quarter and spoke to Lot and said to him: Where are the men who came to you tonight? Let them come out to us that we may rape them.

Lot went out to them in front of the door and locked the door behind him, and begged and strenuously resisted to bring the men out to them, and said: Do not harm these men of God. That is why they came under the shadow of my roof. But they said: Come here. Then they said: Did you not come here simply as a stranger and now want to be judge? Very well, we will do more harm to you than to those men; and they insisted violently against the man Lot. And when they ran up and were going to break down the door, the men reached out and pulled Lot into the house to them and locked the house door. And the men outside the door were stricken with blindness, both small and great, so that they could not find the door.

And the men said to Lot: Do you have besides those here a daughter-in-law or sons or daughters? Take everyone in this city that belongs to you out of this place, for we will destroy this place because their stench is great before the Lord; he sent us to destroy it. Then Lot went out and talked to his sons-in-law who were to marry his daughters: Get up and leave this place, for the Lord is going to destroy this city. But to them it was a laughing matter.

When the dawn came up the angels commanded Lot to make haste and said: Arise, take your wife and your two daughters who are here, so you will not perish in the transgression of this city. When he hesitated the men seized him and his wife and his two daughters by the hand so that the Lord would spare him, and led them out and left them outside the city.

And when they had brought him out they said: Escape with your life. And do not look back and do not stay on the whole plain. Escape to the mountain that you may not perish. But Lot said to them: No, my Lord; behold, since your servant has found grace in your sight, magnify your mercy that you have shown me in preserving my life. I cannot escape to the mountain; I might meet with an accident and I would die. Behold, there is a town to which I can flee, and it is, after all, small, that my soul may live.

Then he said to him: Behold, I have considered you in this matter also, and will not overthrow the town of which you have spoken. Hurry and escape there; for I can do nothing until you get there. Therefore the town is called Zoar. And the sun had risen when Lot entered Zoar.

Then the Lord let sulphur and fire rain down on Sodom and Gomorrah and overthrew the cities, the entire area, and all the inhabitants of the cities and all that had grown on the land. And his wife looked back and turned into a pillar of salt.

But Abraham arose early in the morning and went to the place where he had stood before the Lord and turned his face toward Sodom and looked, and behold, smoke arose from the land like the smoke from a furnace. When God destroyed the cities of the plain he remembered Abraham and led Lot out of the cities that he overthrew, in which Lot lived.

Herewith God has set an example for all who would in the future be ungodly. 2 Pet. 2b.

But the abominations and sins with which the Sodomites sinned so grievously are mentioned by the Prophet Ezekiel, 16e, with the following words as a rebuke to Israel: The sin of your sister Sodom was pride, fullness of food, idleness, sufficiency of everything. Those things she and her daughters had. But besides that they did not aid the poor or the needy and acted abominably in my sight. Therefore I destroyed them as soon as I saw it.

Further, one sees in the Holy Scripture that it was not only the heathen Sodomites and similar peoples who lived and acted wickedly in God's sight, and that God punished them repeatedly and severely, but also that also Israel, which was to have been a people of God, to whom God the Lord even gave his commandments and the law, which they, however, did not keep but frequently transgressed. For the sinful nature inherited from Adam clung to them to that degree, as Esdras testifies in his fourth book, Chapter 3, and says: And your glory has passed through four fiery gates and earthquakes and wind and cold so that you gave the law to the seed of Jacob and zeal to the race of Israel and have not taken away their wicked hearts so that your law could bear fruit in them, for the first Adam bore a wicked heart, transgressed, and was overcome. Yes, and all who are descended from him; the weakness remained in the heart of the people with the law with the wickedness of the roots and has perished. The goodness and the wickedness remained. It still remains in all peoples who have not been born again through God's Word, especially the so-called Christians, who boast of being Christians with their mouths, but have departed from God and come short of the praise that God should have in them. As it is written, Romans 3c: There is none righteous, not even one; there is none that has understanding and asks for God. They have all departed and are altogether unprofitable. There is none that does good, not even one. Their throat is an open grave, with their tongues they practice deceit. The poison of asps is under their lips. Their mouth is full of cursing and bitterness. Their feet are swift to shed blood. In their ways are destruction and transgression, and they have not known the way of peace. There is no fear of God before their eyes.

That even a dead man can better understand how the world and those who with their mouths boast of being Christians have departed so far from the right way, and their life and being is against God, we have abundant indication in the Ten Commandments if one holds them up beside the life and course of the world that they do not at all agree.

(Now continue in the front of this book, p. 73 to pp. 79 and 85.)

SOURCE: Codex 213 (Codex Ritualis), fol. 1r-74r, Slovenská Akademia Vied, Bratislava, ČSSR, compared with Codex G-10-49-93, Státni Archiv, Brno, ČSSR.

REGULATION CONCERNING THE MATCHING OF THE YOUNG PEOPLE FOR MARRIAGE, 1643

[Andreas Ehrenpreis:]

ACCORDING TO THE DECISION OF THE ELDERS, THE FOLLOWING REGULATIONS WERE READ TO THE BROTHERHOOD AT SABATISCH, FEBRUARY 10, 1643[1]

Forced by necessity and a just cause and by no means for our own pleasure, rather because of numerous complaints by many godly people, further since we fear to arouse the wrath and displeasure of the Lord, we therefore feel constrained to investigate a grave matter and to warn the entire brotherhood.

First of all we warn the brotherhood against all disgraceful match-making which is being practiced nowadays so shamefully. Not only the older people, who should be ashamed of this, but younger ones as well are proposing marriage to one another through the intermediary of friends or mere acquaintances. They do this frequently and without any inhibition, carrying letters and messages from house to house, also sending gifts and other favours. These activities contradict all propriety and decency as we know it. They are considered a bad and harmful growth in the house of the Lord which must be weeded out.

Just think what an evil situation it is when an old woman or an impudent young girl goes to this or that brother (or sister) to inform him or her of the marriage proposal of another person. No brother has any such authority, be he old or young, for this is not honourable before God.

The servants of the Word (ministers) are prohibited by our church regulations (*Gemeindeordnungen*) to approve such marriages or to perform

---

1 Translated by Ilse Reist and Robert Friedmann, 1967.

them in private; rather they are to advise our people to place themselves in the hands of God according to our old customs.

Just as the ministers are restrained by our regulations [on marriage], how could we allow all the others to do as they please? Unfortunately, a disorderly practice has developed among us whereby people no longer care to come to our "marriage convocations" unless they know beforehand to whom they will be married.

Courtship, match-making and pushing each other into marriage cause shame and sorrow. Afterwards the one or other regrets it and changes his mind, bringing in addition mockery and disgrace upon one another. It is certainly neither Christian nor brotherly to cheat another fellow-believer. Therefore we will no longer tolerate all these practices.

What is still more wrong is that often one person brings another innocent party into disrepute by groundless accusations. These people lose all fear of God and thus willfully fall into sin. Everyone is well acquainted with the scriptural passages which say: "Him who slanders his neighbour secretly, I will destroy" (Psalm 101:5), or: "The words of the slanderer are sharp arrows piercing the heart" (Prov. 25:18), or: "The lash with the rod causes welts, but the lash with the tongue crushes the bone" (Prov. 25:15).

Some people do not even realize how far they actually have deviated from the [proper] way, and think that they have done only the right thing. Will all those honest people please speak out against such activities, or if such admonitions do not bring results, will they please bring it to our attention, so that sin and frivolity may be stopped.

In some cases people were persuaded to marry a certain person and nobody could make them change their mind. Through false witness some are talked into marriage which they never should have accepted. But because it was this or that person who did the match-making, it was supposed to be a fine deal. Afterwards, people would say: "Too bad for that brother, that he has her—or that she has him—for a spouse." After such a marriage, many a person has become useless in the brotherhood [*Gemein*].

Many a man had to admit later to his own shame and disdain that a certain matchmaker had tricked him into his marriage. "If I only had known it," he would now say," I would never have done it." When afterwards others will laugh about his foolishness, he soon weeps.

These and similar disorderly practices do not only cause a lot of misery, they are above all sinful because people want to marry according to their own will instead of in the fear of God. [The Bible] says of these people that "they looked upon the daughters of man, to see if they were fine, and they chose as their wives whom they wanted" (Genesis 6:2). In such a way the first world became guilty before God, bringing upon the wrath of God and the great flood, and all perished.

Therefore, people have to follow the commandments of the Lord and the examples of the forefathers. They must trust in God and the elders, and must subject their own will to the decisions of the brotherhood. They must not impudently and boldly despise good advice and willfully assume that it has to be this woman or that man and none other. This is not right.

A good example is the servant of Abraham who went to Mesopotamia to get a wife for Isaac. Neither father nor son knew whom the servant would bring home, how she would look and what her name would be. The bridegroom and his father and also the bride's father, mother and brother all had to put their trust in the old servant because neither party knew the other.

In the same manner the God-fearing Tobit followed his guide who, in his eyes, was a mortal being (for he did not know that his companion was an angel). Yet this guide advised Tobit to marry Sarah, the daughter of Raguel. Tobit consented even though he would have had good reasons for misgivings, since Sarah had had seven husbands before who had all been killed, and Tobit could have feared the same fate. But he did not dare to reject his companion's suggestion. Tobit was a fair young man, but he obediently did what he was told to do, and this brought much happiness to him and many blessings in his marriage.

There are many more such examples in Holy Scriptures. In the history of the brotherhood there are even more, as many an older brother or sister still can testify. Many honourable brethren and sisters put themselves into the hands of God when they went to a marriage assembly, not knowing who would become their partner. They would have been ashamed even to think of matchmaking. And yet, these were happier marriages than those who married out of sheer carnal love. But even if things should not always have turned out perfectly for them, their hardships were easier to bear because they knew that they had followed good advice and had not brought it about themselves. They could thus accept their burden perhaps as a test from the Lord.

Therefore it has been resolved that self-will, the arrangement of marriages in the way described above, can no longer be tolerated. Any such arranging of a match beforehand is strictly prohibited among us because nothing good comes of it, as was said before.

This does not mean, however, that we would want to pressure someone of our brotherhood if this person has a good excuse. Such a person can always confide in a God-fearing brother or sister, and no one will take it amiss. But things cannot go on in the disorderly manner as heretofore.

In the olden days nobody would have thought of making such marriage arrangements according to his own pleasure. Today, however, when a person desires to get married in such a way, we [the elders] are expected simply to consent to it and by this to confirm such an unlawful kind of matching. In giving such people into marriage, we thereby testify falsely, inasmuch as we are supposed to say that the couple was married according to the counsel of the elders and the example of the forefathers. Instead, the exact opposite has taken place. One should rather have said [with the Scripture]: "They took those for wives whom they wanted" (Gen. 6: 2).

This then is the regulation which we wanted to make known herewith to everybody in the brotherhood, as a warning so that everyone knows where he stands and that no one acts imprudently and brings unhappiness upon himself. But wherever honour and order prevail, there we will gladly give our help.

There is still another item we want to mention. Old and young are indulging often in disrespectful and dishonourable talk nowadays, with coarse and useless words. They vex young people in this manner, speaking to them of marriage [and thus confuse them]. They should be ashamed about this. Instead of reprimanding and punishing the youth, and teaching them discipline and the fear of God {as was done in the olden days], older people are often themselves guilty of such misconduct. We hear that they gossip and slander others irresponsibly. This is not at all proper for God-fearing people; it spoils the youth and newcomers, and incites them to sinful activities. Consequently young people are talked into marriage much too early, before they even know how to work and how to earn their bread. If these young people had to make their own living they would not even think of marrying at that age.

This entire situation is often promoted by useless chitchat [concerning marriage and the like], be it just for fun or out of unconcern to protect the youth» so that young people may actually hear everything if they care to listen. Even honourable people of the world outside tell their children to leave the room when such things are being discussed. Thus we repeat: may everybody be warned to watch what he says and what he does, and keep in mind that he will have to give account for all this to his Heavenly Father.

Thirdly, we are compelled to speak to you also concerning the Lord's Supper where much disorder has arisen recently. Instead of partaking of it out of devotion and godly zeal for the comfort of the soul, some people give the impression that they prefer rather to run around visiting [at the time of our celebration], carrying messages and doing other errands for this or that reason. All of this is not proper in general, and is particularly improper on the occasion of our celebration of the Lord's Supper. People always have enough reasons to spare no expense or inconvenience just to go to faraway places over water, mountains and valleys, annoying other people by our garb (which covers up our poverty), thus making themselves—and all of us—suspect that they are neither concerned about the Lord's Word nor about his work.

And even though they are advised against, or even refused, such travel, they get so rough and demanding that at last one has to give in. But once they get permission for such travels because of some good cause, others take it to be a general rule, and request the same privilege for themselves.

We ask you not to put us [elders] in such an awkward position which makes our task very hard and difficult. You should rather be much concerned to be deemed worthy and to be prepared [for the Lord's table], that it may serve you as an assurance of your salvation.

SOURCE: A. J. F. Zieglschmid (ed.), *Das Klein-Geschichtsbuch der Hutterischen Brüder* (Philadelphia, 1947), 214-18.

APPENDIX: Sources concerning the traditional marriage practices of the Hutterites:

(1) Peter Riedemann gives the following guidelines in his *Rechenschaft* of 1540 (English ed. 1950, pp. 97-100) in his chapter "Concerning Marriage": "If marriage is to be godly the partners must be married not by their own preference or choosing but under God's leading and direction."

"Therefore it must not be that a person chooses according to the flesh but expects such a gift from the Lord through diligent prayer, that the Lord may send him someone he has chosen for him who would be a blessing for him in his life and his salvation. After such prayer he should ask the elders and not his own flesh that God may show him through the elders whom he has chosen for him. After that he should gratefully accept the one whom the Lord has indicated and sent to him, be the other person young or old, rich or poor."

(2) In 1578, Professor Stefan Gerlach of Tübingen visited his sister at a Bruderhof in Moravia, and afterwards gave the following description: "My own sister Sara did not accept her husband gladly but could not object. For this is the way they arrange their marriages. On a certain Sunday the preachers call the marriageable young men and young women together in one place and line them up in front of each other. They present three young men to a girl. She has to pick one of them. She is not exactly forced to do so yet also not free to act against the will of the preacher, etc." (Gustav Bossert, ed., Täuferakten, Vol. I: *Württemberg*, p. 1107.)

(3) In 1612 the Polish nobleman Andreas Rey of Naglovitz visited a Bruderhof in Moravia and afterwards wrote a letter in Latin to his French friend Philipe du Plessis-Mornay. In it he gives a very dramatic description of the marriage customs of the Hutterites in Moravia at that time. He writes:

> "The girls who are to be given into marriage do not marry the young man whom they would wish to marry or by whom they were asked. Rather they have to take the one destined to them by the lot. For if a young man wants to get

married, he will be shown three girls whom (in many cases) he does not want at all or whom he has never seen before. Of these three he chooses one he prefers.... A number of times during a year they hold marriage [assemblies] at some place previously decided on. Speaking from a sort of platform they call for all those who desire to get married to step forward, both young men and young women. Here they choose each other upon first sight out of groups of three. The preachers will be of some assistance to them since by their prestige they have the power to decide regardless of the preference of the young people. The girl must marry the one the minister decides on. Often the man must take the oldest of the three girls presented to him if she wants him. If the one or the other of the young folks presented to each other does not want to marry the particular person presented, he or she must wait for another six months.

After this procedure, they all are married immediately. Then the men eat with the young husbands, and the young brides with the rest of the women. After the meal each man takes his new wife home."

(František Hrubý, "Die Wiedertäufer in Mähren," *Archiv für Reformationsgeschichte*, XXXII [1935], p. 8.)

(4) The custom to have one's marriage partner picked out by the elders began to lose influence in the seventeenth century. But it was not until the middle of the nineteenth century (around 1845) that the practice was brought to a complete end, due to the intervention of the respected Mennonite Elder Johannes Cornies. See *Kleingeschichtsbuch*, p. 437-38, related in D. H. Epp, *Johann Cornies: Züge aus seinem Leben und seinen Werken*, 1909. A summary is also given in Robert Friedmann, "Marriage, Hutterite," *Mennonite Encyclopedia*, III, 510-11.

—ROBERT FRIEDMANN

THE COMMUNAL DISCIPLINE OF 1651[1]
Annual exhortation of the faithful brethren

Each elder should, as far as possible, gather together all the faithful brethren in his locality. Among those to be called together should be householder, his assistants, the field boss, the purchaser, the distributor, the manager of the wine cellar, the schoolmaster, other foremen and their helpers as well as trusted brethren in the house, such as the manager of the granary, the miller, gardener and carter. (If there should be a person working at a place some distance away, he should be visited and be made familiar with the essentials of the ordinance.)

The following exhortation should be read to them: Jethro's advice [Ex. 18] proved useful to Moses, the servant of the Lord in the desert, namely that he should look around among all the people for honest men, who are God-fearing, truthful and free of covetousness in order to place them over groups of 1000, over 100, over 50 and over 10, so that they lighten his burden by sharing it with him. If Moses would do what the Lord told him, he would be able to carry out God's plan, and the people of Israel would safely reach their destination.

And thus Solomon also teaches (Prov. 11:14): "Where there is no counsel, a people fall; but in an abundance of counsellors there is safety."

You and all the faithful have chosen us to be your shepherds and teachers, and we are charged to watch over the church of God and take care of it as those who must render account. It is earnestly ordered in the law, that if we see our neighbour's ox or donkey go astray or fall down under their load, we must not leave them, but come to their aid.

If then we are called to do that for an ox or a donkey, how much more must we watch over, care for and admonish the sheep of the Lord, yea the children of God who go astray and whose souls might be hurt.

---

1 Source: Zieglschmid (1947), 519-32. A footnote by Zieglschmid states that these regulations were apparently written shortly before October 22, 1651, for they were probably read on that day in the spinning room at Lewar, Slovakia. It can be assumed that Elder Andreas Ehrenpreis (1639-1662) was the author. This discipline is still read periodically in the colonies. Translated by Ilse Reist, edited by Robert Friedmann.

For if the sheep are lost or have gone astray, the shepherds will be sought out and required to give account.

Yet if someone will not accept warning or rebuke in spite of all diligent attempts, his blood will be on his own head and the shepherds will be found without guilt.

And since we see clearly that many in the community are going astray, are soiling their souls and are getting hurt, we consider ourselves compelled before God to do some serious inquiry, to blow the trumpets, to warn of danger and harm, so that we do not end up a rotten and corrupt people like the Israelites who brought on themselves the wrath of God.

Therefore it is our brotherly wish and desire that you, dear brethren, help us according to your own ability to watch over the Lord's own people that you might not say "I am not an overseer, householder or appointed brother." No, not that, but that you too carry the burden of responsibility and be always and everywhere a good example before the people; for a good leader has good followers.

May you and all the brethren, sisters and young people earnestly uphold the Word of God, as it should be, and be decent in everything as it should be.

The sisters should be veiled or wear kerchiefs. There is sometimes much neglect in this. And some give the impression as if they would not care or would not like to practice this any longer. This is the first step towards corruption. As with Adam and Eve, we have the same examples today.

The young ones or everyone able to read should be thoroughly taught the songs, epistles and confessions of the martyred brethren so that our people are more firmly grounded in the articles of faith. If it then should happen that one be imprisoned, or has to give account of his faith that he would know as much about the Lord as he ought to know. We are aware that in such a situation we have nothing left but to trust in the Lord in Heaven. If one of our people would by chance be asked about his faith, there might be some strange answers coming forth.

Out in the world some so-called Christians have special teaching for their children as well as their hired men and women in church on Sundays. How much more should we, the Lord's people, who consider those other groups as false brethren, work towards raising our young in the fear of the Lord, lest we be put to shame by doing the opposite. All of our youth who are able to read and write should be kept in practice, lest they forget it. Others should listen faithfully, whenever spiritual things are read. Such opportunities should always be encouraged. Yet we find that this is not the case.

Our church regulations should be diligently observed at all times, so that sin and lack of discipline, such as illicit relationships, selfishness and other

The Communal Discipline of 1651

forms of dishonesty, particularly theft, do not remain hidden but come out in the open.

What grieves us especially, is the fact that some people among us have their own money. There is buying going on and there is disorder, all founded on greed, which is causing a lot of confusion. There is random buying of all sorts of available items, particularly meat, wine and other food. This in turn leads to undisciplined habits of eating and drinking.

This is the source of much disorder and bitterness. People's appetites are whetted so that they run after money early and late and get caught up in a maze of sin, not even realizing that they are thereby losing the treasure of their salvation.

It is a known fact that many formerly esteemed members of the brotherhood have miserably perished and drowned in wine, and have become misfits and an object of shame and of mockery.

We have observed with distress how covetousness [greed] brings forth sin in many forms. People among us cling to their own money, seek their own advantage and get themselves involved in theft, lies and many other vices.

There are also too many cases in which selfishness has led through various ways to misuse of the property of the brotherhood. Many no longer deal scrupulously with such items as steel, iron, leather, cloth, linen, flax, wool—in summary, all that which is communal property. There are those who seek to improve their own meals with food from the common larder. Later on they say they got these things in an honest way. Instead, they secretly acquired them by stealing, or through various other tricks such as begging, or asking the stewards. The supervisors or foremen are not authorized to give out money; instead, they must try to eliminate this practice and must demonstrate that they keep the money together for the brotherhood. Even though these sinful acts are contrary to our profession and belief, they go on unchallenged like a plant not planted by our Heavenly Father but a weed that must be destroyed.

Because of all this the brotherhood becomes impoverished to an extent that we may have to resort to borrowing money, in fact in some cases we have already done so. Who can now say that it was right for the community to borrow money, while we let its members keep money for their own wine, meat and other selfish purposes? This will never be right in the sight of God!

What more harmful thoughts could be expressed than to tolerate increasingly the practice that those who have money buy what they wish, eat and drink, and dress as they want to, while the rest without means of their own would have to bear the consequences.

For this very reason some of our people have become so choosey in their eating habits that they cook their own meals, because they have their own food and no longer eat the food of the community. They are even getting tired of drinking water and prefer wine instead.

All this leads to trouble, loud or silent complaints, and to much unhappiness among those who do not have anything but must watch the rest enjoying themselves. This situation confirms the word of the apostle when he said that the weak brother will perish for whom Christ had died. [Rom. 14:21?]

May God spare each believer from becoming such a soul-murderer who kills him whom Christ brought to life by shedding his own blood. "Cursed be he who misleads a blind man on the road." (Deut. 27)

Remember the "woes" Christ proclaimed (Matt. 13-16), in fact, Christ goes even beyond that and speaks still more emphatically and becomes more specific.

Therefore, this is not at all a trifling matter, even though people like to think they have perfectly good reasons for such arguments as "What could be wrong with a glass of wine?" It is not this small item that matters here, it is the fact that law and order have been transgressed. And this is indeed very bad.

Adam and Eve had only eaten an apple. and yet forfeited both the image of God and paradise and lost the favour of God. What matters is that a transgression has occurred, and not the object through which the transgression came about.

The man of God only ate bread and drank water, not because of any particular temptation but out of good intentions, and yet he had to die by being devoured by lions.

Esau ate only pottage, but by doing so he transgressed the law, he became an outcast unworthy of the blessing and lost his inheritance. During this year we heard of many such examples in our preaching.

We are not dealing here with man-made laws "by which we seduce ourselves by such perverse liberties," as some tell us. Christ the Lord is speaking clearly enough when he says, "He who hears you, hears me." Paul speaks of the church as of a (strong) rope and foundation of the truth. Christ tells us to regard those as heathen and publicans who refuse to follow the voice of God's people.

We have the example where the first of the seven sons said to the king: We are ready to die for we have sinned against the commandments of God and our forefathers [2nd Book of Maccabees, 7:2]. It is not enough, therefore, to claim that this is simply a law made by man. Our brotherhood has rules which we have all acknowledged and willingly accepted. They are based on the Gospels and Christ's teachings. By virtue of these rules we are forbidden to keep money to ourselves, to buy and trade on our own and to look selfishly after our own affairs.

And even though some of our people may retort with the excuse, "If I were faring as well as you or this or that brother, and if the brotherhood would give me this or that, then I wouldn't need to go after it myself," all should know once and for all that our ordinances were given by God, by Jesus Christ and by the Apostles. If this offends someone, it does so without reason and to their own harm.

They tell us first of all, we should not claim too much liberty and power for ourselves but conduct ourselves in such a way as not to vex others by honours according to our office. [See *Mennonite Encyclopedia*, III, 698-99.) But there are always those who harbour bad feelings against us, as was the case of the Corinthians and the apostle. The Apostle had said to them: "When I preached to you the message of the Gospel, I asked nothing in return, and I never became a burden to anyone of you." This remark was not intended to be a compliment but rather a rebuke.

What was thus ordained by God is shown in the words of the Lord to Moses: "The priests and Levites among the children of Israel shall possess no inheritance, but shall eat of the sacrifices to the Lord." And when Joshua distributed the promised land among all the tribes, he gave nothing to the priests but said: "The sacrifice of the Lord your God is their share, as he has promised them, namely the best animals, which are without blemish, oil and wheat flour and the first fruits." This was their eternal privilege.

Likewise, Christ himself told the apostles what to do when he called them away from their work and sent them out to preach. He said to them: "When you enter a town, market place or house, eat and drink of what they have or what they offer you, for each labourer is worth his keep (food)." This is why he sent them out without money, without sack or bag. And the Jews and the heathen did the same. Shortly before his death Jesus asked his disciples: "How often did I send you out without money, without sack or bag? Have you ever lacked anything?" They answered: "Lord, we never did." This is demonstrated quite powerfully, when the Apostle rebukes the Corinthians, as quoted before.

May these examples serve as answer to those among us who like to accuse us of teaching things we ourselves do not keep, and of being unreasonable in our judgment. Oh, not at all! If these regulations were not ordained by God, if Christ and the apostles, especially Paul, would not have commanded them, and if the Lord's own (church) would not have made such provisions one hundred years ago, we ourselves would never dare to set up such requirements, even though they are not as hard as some think.

There are those among our people today who hardly accept our leadership anymore. Some tell us, we should simply give the people what they are entitled to. This may be well meant, but the fact is, we are living in hard times. We have one meagre year after the other. We hardly can think of wine and meat but are concerned with how to get our daily bread.

Now you will ask, how is it that God sends hunger, want and rising prices? Who can resist his will? Nevertheless, how can we speak of hunger, if none of us lack the daily bread? The people of Israel would not have longed for meat as long as they did not have enough bread and water; but as soon as they grew tired of the bread, they became hungry for meat and other delicacies. But we don't read of any great thirst for wine. The Israelites rather contented themselves for forty years with one kind of food and drink.

From what we can observe today in our brotherhood, people are wearing better clothing and have more things in spite of present hard times than they ever had back in Moravia. There are many among us who still remember how they had to make ends meet there, in all their poverty.

We cannot permit selfishness to rise up again, in spite of such arguments and excuses, and we cannot drop the "Article of the True Christian Community [of goods]," on which our whole concept of life is based. For it so many believers fought and witnessed mightily; they proclaimed it with power; for it they were imprisoned, tortured and killed.

Today we sing their songs and read their epistles, and we laud and praise them highly, and yet we tread under foot their ordinances, their teachings and their wisdom, and we get so far away from all this, that they may become our judges at the last day.

The buying and selling in the Temple of Jerusalem must have looked even more respectable, because people thought they promote worship in this way. But remember Christ's outrage, and how he drove them out of the temple!

There is no basis to this buying, to this profit making and pursuit of self interest; nobody has the right to do that, or anything similar. Nothing but harm and corruption can come of this. Such actions are like baleful thorny thickets, which smother the seed of the divine Word and make people forget God, so that there is no more zeal for God left, particularly among the young people. Some of them no longer want to meditate on the Sunday sermon, or on the Scriptures after work. Neither do they want to practice reading and writing. Instead, each one follows his greed, does what he wants, thinking solely about food and drink, about how to get money, and what to use it for. These people lose the treasure of their salvation, and they do not realize how their spiritual light is going out bit by bit. We are afraid that our youth will stray further from the narrow path, and we will be responsible for it.

It is not enough that we take care of their outward needs, and make them become used to receive their food and drink. From the older people they learn to run after their own money, to buy and to trade. Some parents have already started to give their children money to buy things. Years ago many faithful brethren would have spit out over such a situation. How dare one accustom children to wine and other delicacies, thus enslaving them for the rest of their lives, so that nothing good can come of them. And yet, people think this is all right, and they make fun of the rules of our brotherhood, and allow them to pass with all those practices. If we talk to them about working and about diligence, they speak about eating and drinking. It is, therefore, very urgent to fight such evil growth.

Yet we do console ourselves with the fact that there are still many faithful, honest people among us who are able to testify that they never did any such trading. Among them are those who were hired out; there are supervisors and others who can name persons and places where they never drank wine in their shops in the last two years, even though there were a good number of people working together. And still all did their work properly.

How is it that all of a sudden people become so undisciplined, unable to do anything unless there is wine around. How is it that they can no longer render each other a service, unless there is a good drop of wine, or wine-money. Preachers and stewards seem to know less about this situation than some of their people.

Therefore, all supervisors are charged to see to it, that no harmful weeds can come up which cause all sorts of corruption. They must remember the words of the Apostle in 2 Cor. 6, mentioned before.

Those in responsible positions must guard themselves from becoming a nuisance and bad example. Otherwise they will lose their authority. People will no longer listen to them but defy their orders and say: "If you say that, I'll tell the brother what you did."

If the supervisors know of people who have their own money, they must disclose such cases, otherwise the practice can not be broken. The supervisors must be more concerned to find favour with the Lord in Heaven and to care for the people's salvation and spiritual growth than to seek other persons' favour.

They must not let their women dominate them or let them deal or quarrel with other people. This will provoke the other sisters.

The supervisors must not give money to anyone, be it sister or brother, relative or friend, neither as a token of their favour nor as an occasional tip. Likewise, the supervisors are not free to buy things for themselves or their families, but must get what they need through the brotherhood. They are not allowed to store material supplies for their trade plus cash in addition.

According to the old ordinance, the supervisor should be questioned about money that was either lent out or borrowed by the people. After the reading of this ordinance, each supervisor must report about this matter to the householder in writing. One should guard against lending and taking in pawns, because the pledges are of little value to the individuals and the whole community. Often a person has wasted much by getting into debt, by lending out money and then, trying to collect it. Even though it may look as if he had made a profit, he afterwards got into bad company or lost his good name, took to drinking and cheated our widows and orphans out of their share. According to our ordinance, one has to give an account of one's money dealings every second week.

We have come to the point where we no longer know how to pay for our precious grain (after we have found out how poor we really are). Nevertheless, some supervisors always manage to have a bag full of money. And then they even dare to say: "This will all belong to the church after I die." A fine thing indeed, to hold back one's contribution until death, or to make others wait that long! This is the way the rich worldling leaves his possessions.

Sometimes it happens that after the death of such a brother the wife and children dirty their hands with this money which was kept back selfishly, and they hold on to it and bring shame and corruption on themselves. A man can set a spiritual trap for his family with his greed. Others like him have caused their own downfall, because they hung their heart on money, became rich and proud, sometimes even left the brotherhood. And after that they had very few happy hours and often came to a miserable end.

We must know how much money has been left within the brotherhood. Therefore each supervisor must turn in his money, and rid himself of it, since he is held accountable before God and must not burden himself with it. May each one judge for himself whether it is right that some gather treasures for themselves with the money they take in during their daily work, and that they do this at the expense of the community. Likewise, the supervisors are not allowed to lend money to each other in secret. If someone needs something, he should ask for it. If he is considered to need what he asks for, he will get it. If it is not necessary, he should not ask for it. Whoever transgresses the ordinance in this respect, will be dealt with in all strictness.

Since such dealings are rightly forbidden for supervisors (namely to buy what they want), the same goes for the rest of the people, husband and wife, young and old. Those who hold something in trust are therefore not lords over it, but are considered stewards who must render account.

The Communal Discipline of 1651

It is thus only fitting that all should be honest. Who cannot be truthful in small and temporal affairs, cannot hope for things eternal. The various offices in the community are therefore created for the care of the people, and not as special honours to those who hold these offices.

The cloth-makers and tailors are not allowed to give cloth to our people or to exchange it, but must distribute the material responsibly according to the people's needs. All should make a special effort to be friendly to outside customers, help them with information and be peaceful when they come to us, so that they must not conclude that we are proud, else we are in for persecution and misery. May we continue to find outside-people who are willing to shelter us as in times past. Whatever our work may be, we must do it honestly and faithfully as unto God so that our good reputation which we owe to our forefathers may not be lost. Occasionally we hear things to the contrary. Everyone of us must do his job conscientiously so that the community is not forced to raise prices in order to make out.

Each faithful member must seek truth and honesty in his encounter with all men, high and low.

All supervisors and office-holding brethren must help to watch out for unchristian greed, so that people do not collect all sorts of things, not knowing at the end what or how much they have accumulated, lest moths and rust corrupt it. Even though we do not like to talk about these things, it is yet our teaching that each one must rid himself of superfluous goods for the sake of his own conscience.

Windows, doors, locks, bed frames, chairs and benches must remain in the bedrooms. This was always our rule. For various reasons it is forbidden to remove these objects.

The practice of inheritance remains abolished as of old. In case of death, clothing and bedding are to be returned to the steward. Only books may be distributed according to our decision.

Householder and distributor must watch diligently that nothing is carried away or disappears and that people afterwards buy it with their money.

Above all everyone should guard against pride. Tailors and seamstresses must abide by their rules. The root of evil often lies in things which are of no good use.

The furrier, hatter, tanner and other craftsmen must not sell items to our people. Rather they should continue to distribute their products according to need without involvement of money. They must not turn their shop into a store. People who do private sewing ("in a little corner") must stop this kind of work. As was resolved earlier, boots for children and schoolboys are not allowed.

The purchase of wine and meat by the supervisors without previous counselling and authorization is absolutely forbidden. Transgressions will be dealt with in all seriousness. Neither householder, supervisors, cellar boss or distributors may use property of the community to gain personal favours. Such actions have already caused a lot of unhappiness. And yet, these unlawful practices have become so common among some of us that others are sneered at who strive to keep the rules of the community.

Supervisors must see to it that all work is done well and that customers are not cheated out of their money. It has often been said that a brother is known by the quality of his work and by his diligence. The supervisor, therefore, watches diligently over his people, keeps order among them and pays special attention to the young people so that they are at their shops also on Sundays and holidays. Nobody should give them permission to loiter around in the country. This was never allowed.

A supervisor should take his office seriously and carry out his duties with integrity and honesty in order to insure the respect of others and to be the salt among the people, proving that he has not received in vain the trust of his people and the grace of God.

He should make sure that his workers in the shops do not make a habit out of yelling at each other, of calling each other names and of finding fault. Of course, he must not do it himself either, or the people will say: "I never thought the brother would allow this or do this."

The supervisors should also keep their women folk in check and prevent them from disturbing the peace at the shop or other place of work. The women must not cause annoyance or spend a lot of time with the men in the shops.

Formerly the sisters who carry the water also tended the fire in the shops, such as the cobbler's, tailor's, cooper's, etc. Now it looks as if all the men watch their wives in the shops. And it is often a question what business the women actually have there or whether they keep their men from working.

Once they have gotten this privilege they begin to stay away from the communal eating place (dining hall). Instead, they do their own cooking or take the food to their place. The older brethren will confirm that we never used to have cooking facilities in the shops before. Today, all these different places want their own supply of coal. This is another cause for disorder and annoyance.

Child discipline must be watched over. Some children get very little of it in school. We must not be too lenient with them or they will bear the consequences for the rest of their lives, with some of them becoming so unruly and mischievous that they are practically good for nothing.

The Communal Discipline of 1651

The parents should avoid frequent visits to their bedrooms (living quarters). They should help others to observe these rules. It would not speak well of us if the children of the world had a better reputation than our own.

Therefore, all those in authority must strive to keep order regarding their wives and all the other people—young and old—under their supervision. Let us not ignore the old rules about the upbringing of children, for which our forefathers often paid with their lives. That includes sending the children to school at the proper time. Parents are allowed to keep their children until the age of two, after that period is over, the parents should not wait until they are forced to bring them, as it happens sometimes. It is so much nicer if the children are brought to school voluntarily.

The old ordinance mentions that parents who had to move around were not allowed to take their children along. They were not even allowed to request such a privilege. If the parents gave evidence of having too much fleshly attachment to their children, they were separated from them to insure the proper upbringing of the infants. For we have to fear the Lord that he would punish us for such fleshly weakness. We don't want to be unduly hard in cases of particular need. We see how many of these undisciplined, ill-bred children turn into grown-ups who cause hardships for the brotherhood, some of them even disappear, they turn into good-for-nothings and come to a sad end. We don't want to blame anyone in particular for this.

Some parents may say they don't want to be hard on their small children while they are still with them, assuming that the children will get enough physical punishment once they are in school. Afterwards these parents are constantly running to school and interfering with the disciplining of their own and other school children. How can the teacher discipline properly if there are persons present who do not belong in school.

Our people must not unnecessarily walk about in the fields or at other places. This is especially improper before the church service on Sunday. During the sermon one should not open the door for every trivial reason and call this or that brother out of the service unless there is a pressing matter which needs to be taken care of immediately. Look at the world.

All supervisors must keep their eyes on the bread. Nobody should give bread away, be it to beggars or other people. This simply encourages the beggars to roam around more freely in our houses and rooms. If some of us had to look out for ourselves these days to make a living, we would not handle bread so carelessly. It would not be sufficient for him to say, "Oh, I still have to pay for that loaf of bread." The same goes for the use of candles. A supervisor can waste a lot of candles if he is not careful. The people must make an effort to light and to extinguish the candles carefully. The supervisors must be thrifty with the candles and not give them away.

Our people are again reminded that nobody is allowed to raise his own pigeons, chicks, rabbits, etc.

When an evildoer is being executed in public, our folks should not run to such places to look on. (They might experience mockery there inasmuch as we do not cooperate otherwise with those people.) Brothers and, above all, sisters are not allowed to go to market, unless the brothers have business there.

Witchcraft, magic and fortune-telling, whether pronounced on men or beast, are absolutely forbidden in the community. And anyone knowing about such a case is responsible to make it known. Such practices are banned in both the Old and the New Testament. Banishment and other punishment must be used within the community, otherwise we cannot be God's people.

Whatever disobedience there may be among young or old, it must not be tolerated. There has to be punishment, for the world does not tolerate disobedience either. When it comes to either a brother or sister, young or old, one should do it with devotion and reverence and must never appear laughing or start gossiping, which makes it rather bad and is not even done by the world.

The brethren should give testimony against sin and wrongdoing before the entire brotherhood. They should witness [to their faith] with zeal and diligence and should not be pushed to do so. For it is more convincing than the other way round. Such a testimony does not need many words and may be called a real or genuine testimony.

It is a shame that so often transgressions need to be itemized. We are sometimes at a loss of what to think of this. Afterwards our people gossip about it.

Shunning is not much observed any more. When we tell our people to avoid those who have fallen away, some of our brethren and sisters defy our orders and tell the apostates who then become our enemies and threaten us. This is an intolerable and sad situation. We are talking here only about those guilty of this transgression and we want them to be watched. Most of the apostates have become so because of the appetites of their bellies. They know very well what they hanker after.

How can we trust those [in the brotherhood] who take our way so easy and thus endanger us instead of helping us? In olden days when they noticed that a brother or elder was in danger they would have stepped right in for him.

One should not run around with the people of the world and accept gifts from them. For they expect that these gifts will be paid back, and this is not fitting for a believer. Such relationships have often caused irritation and unhappiness. Many have been led astray through them.

There are supervisors and brethren who live away from the community proper, such as the millers, gardeners and dairymen, etc. Some of these people make brandy all year long, consuming most of it with their relatives. A similar thing happens with lard, flour and other items; they disappear instead of being turned in to the community.

There are also some of us here who are too much involved with cattle raising and brandy making. Then the authorities take it all away and the community gets little or nothing from it.

The people must guard against making debts borrowing or lending money. If they were on their own, they wouldn't do it. Now that they have given all they possess to the Lord, they have even less authority to use money as they wish, for it is not theirs any longer. Each brother should therefore turn in what he has to the proper place within the community, so that the needy among us can be taken care of. Let the unbelievers take care of themselves and let not our people lend to them or borrow from them, as it has happened from time to time.

Those of our people who live away from the community should turn in what they produce to the community and they should be content with the usual food, drink and clothing regulations of the community and should not set up for themselves special rules which would alienate them from the rest of our people.

After all, those of our members living on isolated farms bring their children to our bruderhofs. They also bring their sick and their new mothers, and those older people who can no longer work. This is all as it should be. Therefore they should also faithfully turn in all their possessions.

All those of us in places of authority together with the faithful brethren should handle the community's property while being aware of their own responsibility to God, remembering the needy among our people and especially the young brethren that these may learn from them thrift and not careless wastefulness. Selfishness and disorderliness must not be tolerated. The sisters should be encouraged to spin and to work diligently.

The householder and his helpers, the field boss and all supervisors in the house and on the farms must encourage the people to go to worship (*Lehr*) and to set a good example, remembering how their forefathers braved rain, snow and flood, night and cold weather to gather for worship.

There is one more word to say to the brethren who serve as night watchmen in the house and at the gates that they should be more aware of the importance and responsibility of their job. Since all our property is entrusted to them and since all our people go to bed knowing that they will be taken care of by these brethren, they must do their work well.

The watchmen are privileged—and rightly so—to rest and sleep during the day so that they can keep watch at night, when the rest of our people sleep. The men must be alert to ward off danger. It would be a serious offence if they were found sleeping when something did happen.

The watchmen have authority to forbid any unallowed activities at night, such as secret use of fuel and candlelight, as has happened frequently in the absence of the householder and his assistants. There was also cooking and washing going on during the night, as well as soap-making and other unauthorized activity. If the watchmen meet resistance, they must tell the supervisors. But if they know of such activities and tolerate them, the watchmen are subject to discipline, for they are not only the trustees of the whole compound, but of cattle, of fire and of light as well.

The gates must be closed promptly and the house locked to keep intruders out during the twilight. When the gates stand open too long, someone may want to carry something out of the house; he may have planned this during the day. From time to time this has happened. If someone comes to the gate after it was closed, the night watchmen are authorized to ask this person where he had been and what he had been doing so long. If there is something not quite right about it, the watchmen should counsel together, and not keep silent about it.

The night watchmen should keep also an eye on the young people that they do not stay out or run around too long outside the gates, and then by their yelling bother others, be that in the sleeping quarters or in the yard. To avoid unfortunate incidents the watchmen should inform the brethren of disorderly conduct among young or old, such as standing around idly, walking around together, becoming too intimate with one another, etc.

We had people in a house who knew or had seen such behaviour but lacked the courage to take proper action, or simply did not care. This is wrong, and such persons are not free of the charge of neglect.

We don't want you to think that we try to make up new regulations. We are simply upholding the old ordinances and all that for which many of our brave brethren and sisters in the faith have paid with their lives and are resting now in peace.

Therefore, we all must apply ourselves diligently to cleanse the church of God to the best of our God-given ability from those who are useless, so that Jerusalem, the church of God, may be that city where all band together, where all fare well, where all love one another as is testified in the Scriptures;

The Communal Discipline of 1651

may we also follow the example of the God-fearing Tobias, who even though he was in faraway lands did not stray from the path of righteousness.

We hope therefore that we will faithfully abide by all that is good, not preferring the favour of man to that of God, even though some of us fear that unbelievers will not appreciate what we say. All that was announced before you today is nothing new. It is in accordance with the Word of God and the laws of our beloved forefathers.

At the same time we would not dare to present to you this ordinance without counsel and divine guidance. May the community of God be cleansed from all ungodliness as Jacob was cleansed, and may our reward be great in Heaven!

As with Abraham, we charge our people to keep the commandments of the Lord to do what is right and acceptable, knowing that the Lord in his mercy will not withhold from us his will; he will reward all believers, punish the unbelievers, and give us eternal life. This is our desire for ourselves and for all true believers through Jesus Christ, his beloved son, Amen.

We ask all the faithful to remember that we seek nothing hereby, but to praise God, to assure the welfare of the brotherhood and the salvation of each member. We do not want to bring the wrath of God as a punishment on us for our lack of discipline and obedience. The Lord is speaking to us on this subject through his prophet Amos. It says there that the Lord will take up his sword against those who ignore his sacred commandment (Sap. 7). May we also learn from the words of the famous hero Mattathias who said this to his sons (1 Mak. 2:50, 51): Now therefore, my sons, be ye zealous for the law and give your lives for the covenant of your father; call to remembrance what acts our fathers did in their time; so shall ye receive great honour and everlasting name. And for those who love the laws of God and the ordinances of His people, the brotherhood, and who seek their own souls' salvation, may they give testimony and evidence that they are in agreement with the ordinances of the early Church and our community. May they declare whether they still accept that which they have promised on their knees in the covenant of their baptism, and whether they will return to this discipline and abide by it, and let go of all disorder. We ask that each one speak up and tell us.

The earth is full of sinners. They have transgressed and rendered powerless the eternal covenant (Esdras 24), and therefore the curse will swallow up the earth, for its inhabitants have sinned. Therefore will they burn, and there will be few who are left.

Those who agree with the church, may they uncover their hearts and declare openly how they stand.

Your speech shall be yes or no. And if someone has a complaint to bring up, he may talk to us alone in confidence.

THE BARBER-SURGEON ("BADER") DISCIPLINE OF 1654

The "Bader-Ordnung" was read to the barber-surgeons in order that they more diligently follow this ordinance. This indicates the serious corruption of that trade, and the attempt by Ehrenpreis to restore its good reputation.[1]

The barber-surgeons are charged

1. To be more mindful of their vocation, of their own souls' salvation and the good and welfare of the brotherhood;

2. To be an asset to their profession and to their faith by showing honesty, faithfulness, industriousness, and sobriety in their work within the brotherhood and for people of whatever class outside the community;

3. To pray faithfully to God, that he will give them grace and bless them and their medication and treatment;

4. To diligently study in the Holy Scriptures and the books of pharmacy;

5. To rise promptly in the morning at reveille, and to retire in good time at night and to avoid all disorderliness;

6. Not to leave their "shop" without previous notice;

7. To go where they are sent and faithfully carry out their instructions;

8. To gather roots and herbs as instructed, and not to come home empty-handed, because their time was spent in sloth or wine drinking.

9. Not to loiter around in the house or in the workshops, gossiping or socializing, and causing annoyance; likewise not to sit and drink with the people of the world and to show approval of this, as some have been doing. It is not right to be so deceitful!

10. To befriend all people and not to give curt answers and make sarcastic remarks. The latter is exceedingly disgraceful for us.

---

[1] This interpretive introduction is from Josepf Beck, *Die Geschichtsbücher der Wiedertäufer...* (Vienna, 1883), 485; the original German text is also found in Beck, pp. 485-87. Translated by Ilse Reist.

11. NB. NB. Also, do not dress in the style of the world lest you be—as has already happened—not recognized, but greeted and welcomed as a stranger. (NB. disgraceful headdresses and hair.) When people joined the community, they were ashamed of their worldly clothes. Now, some are ashamed to wear the garb of the community. They want everything to look different, be it hats, ribbons, trim, skirt or jacket, belt with either an enormous buckle or just a band, buttons in the back; it is not altogether in the style of the world, yet it must be about half and half.

12. The same goes for manners and speaking: worldly and pompous, hair looking like bristles, scraping with their feet, and other frippery. What a mockery! Certainly the noblemen have enough courtiers around them. (The barber-surgeons must cut the brethren's hair in the proper way, and not according to each individual's taste, such as halfway down to the shoulders and parted in the middle. That is the style of the soldier, and puts our men on the same level with the world. Some of our people have recently shown such disobedient behaviour.)

13. The apprentices must not be led to such arrogance in pompous appearance and other things, lest they be hardly able afterwards to serve the simple peasant with a haircut or washing.

14. The barber-surgeons must keep their instruments immaculately clean and sharpened, so that the peasants would not have to shed tears during a haircut, bloodletting or cupping.

15. In the bath-house the barber-surgeons are to be friendly and take good care of the people. They are not to make people sit and wait. They must not leave the bath-house or barbershop and gossip, while the customers leave in dissatisfaction, as has been happening these days.

16. They are not to avoid work as if they were too good for it or not made for it.

17. They are not supposed to have their own pharmaceuticals and make profit from them.

18. They are not allowed to have their own chickens and pigeons, etc.

19. All money, be it a gift or tip, or be it earned income, must be faithfully handed over to the supervisor.

20. All buying, exchanging and trading must cease and is forbidden, as it always has been in the community.

21. The barber-surgeons must not take money or gifts from those of their clients who belong to our communities, for this is not right!

The Barber-Surgeon Discipline of 1654

22. They must diligently care for our elderly invalids, so that these do not have to sigh and complain.

23. They must not bring their superiors into disrepute or talk behind their backs when conversing with clients, intimating that they could help if only the supervisors would let them have certain medicines.

24. Extreme care must be taken in the administering of medicine, lest they have the patients' blood upon their hands.

25. No barber-surgeon is to set up his private business or independently seek the employment of a nobleman.

26. No one must leave his master (employer) for unjust reason.

27. The barber-surgeons should go regularly to the common dining room along with all the other brothers and sisters. These instructions were also given to the alchemists in Nikolsburg (Mikulov) and to Stophel Eckstain and Nathaniel Hamer. Also, the barber-surgeons must not get too dependent on riding or driving, especially those men who are still young and healthy.

28. They must not become greedy for all sorts of things, like coats and other clothing for themselves and their wives.

29. The older barber-surgeons are to instruct the young ones diligently and to keep them disciplined and respectful. They must not beat the boys, tussle with them or scold them with coarse insults. Likewise, they must not be silly with them and joke with them. The same goes for the barbers' attitudes toward newcomers.

30. If a brother is told of his bad behaviour, he should not immediately want to get up and leave, but accept the reprimand graciously.

31. The barber-surgeons must not collect a lot of superfluous equipment to gratify their own vanity, for they can hardly load all this on their wagon. The barber-surgeons have always had their ordinances! Today, their attitude mocks their honourable forbearers who gave these ordinances and who had decided that the barbers must not travel with too much baggage from one place to another, and must not have more than one wagonload.

What is this leading to? It cannot be tolerated! Suppose a purchaser, householder, man in charge of the dairy, or miller would want to travel around like this; how many wagons would they have to take with them?

And what they (the barber-surgeons) cannot take along they sell, even their domestic animals! – Well, well, what a miserable reputation this gives the community!

32. And when they find that they have situated themselves comfortably, they no longer want to travel, but hang on to their noble employers (*Herrschaft*). They obtain positions of power and thus exercise their own will which is totally in contrast to their calling and commitment.

The fact that the young people are so spoiled, bold, disobedient and insubordinate has not a little to do with this situation.

www.ingramcontent.com/pod-product-compliance
Lightning Source LLC
Chambersburg PA
CBHW031424290426
44110CB00011B/509